Speaking for the Polis

Studies in Rhetoric/Communication
Thomas W. Benson, Series Editor

Speaking
for the Polis

Isocrates' Rhetorical Education

Takis Poulakos

UNIVERSITY OF SOUTH CAROLINA PRESS

Published in Columbia, South Carolina, by the
University of South Carolina Press

Manufactured in the United States of America

01   00   99   98   97   5   4   3   2   1

Library of Congress Cataloging-in-Publication Data

Poulakos, Takis.
    Speaking for the polis : Isocrates' rhetorical education / Takis
Poulakos.
        p.   cm. — (Studies in rhetoric/communication)
    Includes bibliographical references and index.
    ISBN 1–57003–177–0 (cloth)
    1. Isocrates—Criticism and interpretation.   2. Speeches,
addresses, etc., Greek—Greece—Athens—History and criticism.
3. Community life—Greece—Athens—History.   4. Athens (Greece)—
Social conditions.   5. Education, Greek—Greece—Athens.
6. Rhetoric, Ancient.   7. Oratory, Ancient.   I. Title.   II. Series.
PA4218.P68   1997
885'.01—dc21   97–4865

To John Poulakos
μετὰ τῆς εὐσέβειας καὶ τῆς εὐγνωμοσύνης

Contents

Editor's Preface   ix

Preface   xi

Acknowledgments   xiii

Introduction   1

1. Rhetoric and Social Cohesion: The "Hymn to Logos"   9

2. Speaking Like a Citizen: Citizenship, Leadership,
   and Community in *Nicocles*   26

3. Human Agency   46

4. Eloquence and Reflection: *Antidosis*   62

5. Public Deliberation: *Panegyricus*   78

6. Educational Program   93

Conclusion   105

Notes   107

Works Cited   117

Index   125

Editor's Preface

In *Speaking for the Polis*, Takis Poulakos rereads and revives the rhetorical teachings of Isocrates, a Greek orator and teacher of rhetoric who lived from 436 to 338 B.C. Professor Poulakos sees in the surviving works of Isocrates a depiction of rhetorical education as preparation for life and leadership in Athenian politics that has special relevance for the needs of contemporary citizens.

Professor Poulakos argues that Isocrates described rhetoric as the engine for creating unity out of diversity and the public good out of individual action. By its very nature rhetoric appeals to communal values, interests, and desires, stimulating the arts of civilized life. An appropriate education in rhetoric would stimulate adherence to standards that would judge an orator not by the ability to achieve individual ends but rather by the ability to maintain a social order in which citizenship can flourish. Hence, rhetoric is properly seen not as the study of techniques for creating effects upon ignorant hearers, but rather as the study of the proper means by which to create civilization itself. Public deliberation is found in the actions of both speakers and listeners as deliberating agents. Despite the essential optimism and high ideals of this vision, Professor Poulakos does not depict Isocrates as a naive dreamer. Rhetoric always existed in a series of tensions between unity and diversity, personal ambition and the public good, political equality and social-economic inequality, and only proper understanding and proper action could hope to achieve the public good. At the same time, Professor Poulakos himself, whose admiration of Isocrates is deep and subtle, never loses sight of what he calls the situated, political, and provisional nature of Isocrates' views, adapted as they were to another time and place.

Speaking for the Polis is at once a profound rereading of Isocrates situated in ancient Athens and a moving evocation of a rhetoric adapted to the cultural situation of contemporary readers.

Thomas W. Benson

Preface

I first conceived this book as a close study of Isocrates' educational treatises, *Antidosis* and *Against the Sophists*. But the closer I read the *Antidosis*, the more convinced I became that Isocrates' rhetorical education cannot be confined to a study of his instruction in rhetoric. The very spirit of the *Antidosis* seems to me to be offering a critique against any type of education that remains impervious to everyday practices as well as to be making an effort to link his own educational program with political life in Athens. It was the *Antidosis* itself, then, that pushed me away from writing the close study I was prepared to write.

Yet, once the context is opened up, there seems to be no end to what could be included and brought to a reading of *Antidosis* or an understanding of Isocrates' rhetorical education. The Isocratean corpus is immense; no one book could ever capture the breadth of his thought, his practices, his educational activities. I ultimately chose in this work to concentrate on the ways in which Isocrates sought to construct his students' understanding of themselves: the responsibilities they had to themselves as thinkers, to their fellow citizens as human beings, to the tradition of rhetoric as speakers, to the history of their city as potential leaders, and, finally, to their polis as political beings. Comprehension of the uniqueness of Isocrates' rhetorical education, I feel, is possible only through close examination of his efforts to guide his listeners' self-understanding as political and moral agents.

It was the attempt to capture the self-understanding that Isocrates demanded of orators-to-be that not only led me through his enormous corpus but also helped me deal with my present biases as a modern reader. I have not always had that tolerance when faced with Isocrates' own politics. However, once I was able to see the great difference between Isocrates' personal sympathies and party politics and his deeper commitment to political agency, I was successful in suspending the former and focusing on the latter. If our political perspective on Isocrates' rhetoric remains nar-

rowly conceived, we are bound to find in his rhetorical education nothing
of significance to our own historical-cultural moment. However, if we
conceive the political broadly, as an essential aspect of our being, there is
much there to enrich our own understanding and teaching of rhetoric. It
is in this sense that I understand Isocrates' rhetoric as a rhetoric of unification and in this same sense that I understand his rhetorical education as
the art of speaking for the polis.

Acknowledgments

I am grateful to Michael Leff, Kathleen Welch, Victor Vitanza, and Jane Sutton for their sustained and generous support; to Donovan Ochs, Sharon Crowley, George Kennedy, David Konstan, and John Finamore for their caring criticism of various aspects of my work; and to Tom Kane, Dennis Moore, Fred Antczak, Bonnie Bender, and Doug Trank for their professional and personal support.

Speaking
for the Polis

Introduction

At a time when interest in rhetoric and its history is higher than ever before, a study of Isocrates' rhetoric can serve at least two purposes. First, it can expand the discursive horizon of the well-known debate between Plato and the Sophists by making the point that classical Athenian rhetoric was much more than an either/or proposition. Second, it can stimulate our own thinking on the quality of our political life by giving us a portrait of another culture and another time in which the art of rhetoric was called upon to address and resolve problems of division and unity, fragmentation and consolidation, diversity and cooperation—in other words, problems extremely pertinent to our own times. At stake in the first instance is our understanding of the relationship between rhetorical education and political culture; in the second instance, it is our rethinking of the role we wish to assign to rhetorical education today, in our efforts to shape the future direction of our own political culture.

Only a few decades ago Isocrates was fixed, seemingly permanently, in the company of the Attic orators and was understood as a representative of the tradition of civic eloquence.[1] The disciplinary preoccupation with political philosophy and political theory, and the immensely satisfactory outlet this preoccupation could find in Plato and Aristotle, kept Isocrates in the background. Neither a political philosopher nor a political theorist, Isocrates placed a premium on practical knowledge and situated commitments in the domain of the political, which did not always sit well with disciplinary approaches and concerns. What kept Isocrates alive behind mainstream scholarship and its insistence on disciplinarity were the handful of classical scholars whose commitments to a well-rounded liberal education and approaches to learning as an integrated study in the humanities rather than as disciplinary knowledge drove them to Isocrates' broad framework of rhetorical education. Through the pioneer efforts of Kenneth Freeman, Werner Jaeger, Frederick Beck, Henri Marrou, and George Kennedy, Isocrates was carried forth to our own times.[2]

From scholars of rhetoric he did not receive a great deal of attention either. Aristotle drew all scholarly interest, as his *Art of Rhetoric* continued to provide the legitimate origins that the recently reemerging discipline of rhetoric needed. The few inquiries into pre-Aristotelian rhetoric focused on the fierce antagonism between Plato and the Sophists—in an effort either to sharpen rhetoric's identity by opposition to philosophy[3] or, as John Poulakos did, to claim for rhetoric a more spacious home than the one Aristotle had built.[4] As these initial efforts happened to coincide with the "linguistic turn," a host of other scholars joined in and took up the vast potential of sophistic rhetoric to respond to the new challenges brought by poststructuralism.[5] Between the recurring need for ancient authority and the present enthusiasm with the complex relation of language to power and difference, between Aristotle and the Sophists, Isocrates was once again kept, with few exceptions, in the background.[6]

One notable exception was Michael McGee's essay some ten years ago, an essay that captured Isocrates' potential to provide a powerful critique against canons of disciplinarity and ivory-tower approaches to the Academy.[7] In a sense, this book is an attempt to extend that effort. But it is also written out of the conviction that Isocrates' interdisciplinary approach to rhetorical education is only symptomatic of a larger commitment on his part, namely, to link rhetorical education with the affairs and concerns of the polis and to mobilize the art of rhetoric for the purpose of improving the internal conditions of the polis.

Given the sharp contrast between the conditions of Classical Athens and conditions at present, a study on Isocrates may be readily dismissed as altogether irrelevant to our own needs and desires. Classical Athens was a slave society, a place where Athenian women and non-Athenian-born males were noncitizens and where a few landowners and aristocrats maintained a stranglehold on the economy while the majority of people worked fields in the country, lived as manual laborers, or depended on the public treasury for sustenance. It was a society driven by war, expansion, conquest, and people who understood as an assertion of their own freedom the capacity to extend their borders outward and dominate others by turning them into slaves or imposing on them tributes. From the point of view of our own social values and present commitments to equality, there seems to be no connection at all, no reason whatsoever to study Classical Athens or to expect any similarities between society then and now. From that point of view, the only sensible reason to study the Athenians seems to be to celebrate our differences from them or to express our indignation against the economic, racial, and gender inequalities they subscribed to. This point of view shaped some of my earlier work on Isocrates.[8]

Yet my ongoing study of Classical Athens has made me increasingly more sensitive to the differences within that society—differences that tend to be covered over by a perspective that continues to assess the past on the basis of valuations at present.[9] Isocrates' argumentative prose is a constant reminder to modern readers of the intellectual differences that existed at the time in approaches to education as well as in educational objectives and purposes of existing fields of study.[10] And these differences in general education or in rhetorical education frequently turn out to be but manifestations of greater differences still—in ethical, social, and political outlooks.[11] The citizens of Athens were not of one voice as to the direction of their city.

What sustains my interest in Isocrates now is my fascination with the way he sought to navigate around these differences—sometimes respecting or promoting them, other times erasing or conflating them—and carve out a common purpose, a shared view of the cardinal importance of the polis and its welfare, and a concerted effort to make the vitality and destiny of the polis every citizen's affair. It was to that purpose that Isocrates devoted his instruction and for the sake of that purpose that he changed the art of rhetoric from the way it was when he inherited it. The version of rhetoric he left behind is, unequivocally, a rhetoric for the polis.

This seems to me to be a project pertinent to our own times, for the recent emphasis on difference and diversity has made apparent to us the need to think through unity and plurality in new ways, that is, ways that account for, as well as promote, difference and diversity. Even as the need to make the case for the significant role differences play in the production of ideas and the conduct of praxis is far from over, there exists the further need to explore the difficulties involved with unification. The problem is a rhetorical one: how to orchestrate differences in a manner that makes concerted action possible; how to form a genuine "we" out of diversity.[12] To be sure, Isocrates does not provide any solutions to our condition; he confronts another set of problems and inherits another rhetorical tradition. Still, I find it worthwhile to initiate a transaction with the past, especially a moment in the past that illustrates rhetoric's potential to take up problems we are interested in addressing. Isocrates' gift to us, then, may amount to nothing more than an inspiration: that this flexible and pliable art we call rhetoric may be bent and flexed until it responds to our context-specific needs and helps us discover the available means of persuasion in our own situation at present.

In this book I attempt to follow the various ways in which Isocrates changed the rhetorical tradition in order to rescue rhetoric from the ill repute it had received by the time it reached his day; to examine how the changes he made might have provided satisfactory responses to some of

Plato's attacks on rhetoric; to show that these changes amounted to a radically new version of rhetoric and an innovative program in rhetorical education; and, most important, to show that the changes made were political—political not in the narrow sense of party politics but in the broader sense of care and concern for the general welfare. I consider such an inquiry to be indispensable to the modern reader's understanding of Isocrates' rhetorical education as well as to the student of rhetoric, for the contributions he made to the art of rhetoric concern not so much the body of knowledge comprising the field at the time as the possibilities he opened up concerning the uses of art and the ends to which it could be put. And since the new possibilities he created for the art of rhetoric are not always articulated in his educational treatise, I draw on his practice as a rhetorician as much as I consult his discourse as an educator. As I understand it, then, an inquiry into Isocrates' rhetorical education cannot proceed formalistically but must be equally attentive to what he says and to what he does.

It is my contention that the single most important change Isocrates effected in the rhetorical tradition was to give the art of rhetoric a distinctly political orientation. Indeed, this book will advance the argument that under Isocrates rhetoric assumed a character and a purpose congruent with the political practices of the times. In Isocrates' hands rhetoric became the art of politics. The inquiry undertaken in the following pages will focus on the ways in which Isocrates formulated and practiced his art so as to give rhetoric a unique relation to political deliberation; how he looked to pressing issues of the day for rhetoric's subject matter and to the welfare of the polis for the art's end; how he adjusted rhetoric so as to address successfully issues of vital importance to the citizenry and deliberate effectively questions of public policy; and how he mobilized his version of rhetoric in order to advocate courses of action that safeguarded the interests of the citizens and promoted the general welfare of the city-state.

This work will also examine how rhetorical education under Isocrates became an education in deliberating the destiny of the polis. The inquiry will be guided by Isocrates' own assertion that his instruction in rhetoric was but an apprenticeship to active participation in the affairs of the polis and requisite training for effective leadership in Athenian politics. We will scrutinize his claim that his version of rhetoric was equipped to respond to sociopolitical demands for collective representation and that his students were educated in assuming a perspective from which the collective interests of citizens could be represented. Particular attention will be paid to the ways his instruction prepared his students to position themselves within that perspective, to deliberate issues from that standpoint, and to advocate courses of action from that angle. In short, we will examine how under his direction rhetorical education confronted the problem of teaching students how to speak for the polis.

To be sure, these are themes already made familiar to students of Isocrates by scholars before me, especially Jaeger and Kennedy. What I hope to accomplish beyond the existing literature is a sharper focus on Isocrates' rhetoric and rhetorical education. I seek to obtain this focus by bringing to my study, and indeed to every stage of my inquiry, the following interrelated concerns: Isocrates' indebtedness to and departure from the rhetorical tradition, especially Protagoras and Gorgias; his relation to Plato, especially the extent to which his departure from the rhetorical tradition may be regarded as response to Plato's critique of rhetoric; the relation of his version of rhetoric to the social, political, and economic conditions of Athens at the time; the uniqueness of his version of rhetoric in relation to contemporary practices of rhetoric, especially in the context of political deliberation in the assembly; the relation of his rhetorical education to contemporary teachers of rhetoric and other educators; and, finally, the pertinence of his version of rhetoric and his teaching of rhetoric to present rhetorical and pedagogical concerns. These are the general concerns I have brought to the study of Isocrates' rhetoric, and it is through the lens of their combined trajectory that I have tried to examine every major issue along the way.

I begin this study by examining Isocrates' effort to disassociate rhetoric from its reputation as a tool for individual self-advancement and to associate rhetoric instead with social interactions and civil exchanges among human beings. The first chapter locates this effort in the "Hymn to Logos," in which Isocrates praises logos for its contribution to civilized life and its capacity to create social bonds. Showing civilized life to be a result of concerted efforts and collective deliberations, Isocrates exalts logos as maker of unity and guide to unification—a force which brings people together under a common end and a shared set of values, and which shapes their self-understanding as agents of their own destiny through their participation in political deliberation. The exaltation of logos already suggests a different conception of political deliberation than the one typically practiced in the Athenian assembly, for it casts political deliberation, not as an act of public policy advocated by a single individual and approved by the masses, but as a collective practice involving communal inquiries into means as well as ends, into political solutions as well as ethical commitments. Once understood as collective inquiry into the good and the possible of the polis, political deliberation requires a speaker whose individual voice partakes of communal values, interests, and desires and can somehow also represent the larger collectivity. As recast by the hymn to logos, political deliberation can only ensue from the voice of the citizen.

If in order to deliberate the good and the possible of the polis one must speak like a citizen, then we must determine what conditions an orator must meet so as to speak as citizen rather than as individual. This is the inquiry that chapter 2 undertakes by taking a close look at *Nicocles*. Isocrates' advice to the Cyprian king conflates good leadership with citizenly conduct, and effective oratory with the kind of conduct that helps maintain a social order that in turn safeguards the freedom of members of the community to pursue their interests and desires. Borrowing Protagoras' link of rhetorical education to citizenship and adjusting that link to the socio-economic conditions of his day, Isocrates reformulates citizenship as legal/moral conduct that is essential to the structural integrity of the polis. Borrowing from prevalent discourses of moral conduct in his day, Isocrates draws a sharp contrast between citizenly and uncitizenly behavior, as regards both the conduct of Athenians in the polis and the conduct of the Athenian empire toward its allies. This schema, in turn, provides the basis for his argument that existing oratorical practices are the results of uncitizenly conduct: orators in the court and the assembly speak as individuals rather than as citizens, their words being attached to private socio-economic pursuits outside their identity as political agents.

Chapter 3 casts the problem of being able to assume the perspective of a citizen as a problem about human agency. The division drawn between the citizenly and the uncitizenly, along with the accompanying oppositions that this division suggests—between legitimate and illegitimate socio-economic pursuits, reason and emotions, self-restrained and uncontrolled desire—brings us face to face with structural oppositions inherent in the polis. Because the democratic polis was shaped from the start by a political equality and a socio-economic inequality, a member of the polis was unavoidably the direct product of a tension that remained unresolved from generation to generation. Moreover, this was also a tension reflected readily in the two conceptions of rhetoric Isocrates inherited from Protagoras and Gorgias. Occupying the position of a citizen required for Isocrates that the tension between political equality and socio-economic inequality be resolved. Speaking as a citizen similarly required that the tension between Protagoras' and Gorgias' conceptions of rhetoric be resolved. The chapter ends by showing Isocrates' efforts to resolve this dual problem through a discussion of the speaker's character, a discussion that offers a unique portrait of human agency. Accordingly, the question of human agency is resolved when an orator answers to reason or desire, uses self-restraint or indulgence, moderation or excess, only in accordance to the needs of the polis; pursues fame and glory only in regard with earning a good reputation in the polis; and accrues social and economic benefits only as a result of having earned a good reputation.

In the meantime, the speaker's drive to establish a good reputation (and the relation between speaker and audience that such a drive presumes) can no longer be understood as a practice belonging solely to the fifth-century paradigm of rhetoric as a means for self-representation. While rhetorical practices in the fifth century flourished only insofar as they responded to the dynamics of self-representation created by the structure of the democratic courts and the assembly, rhetorical practices endorsed by Isocrates directed rhetoric away from the courts and the assembly and toward public deliberation—a form of political deliberation no longer tied to the technical requirements of making policy in the assembly. It is in this shift, in this interruption of the long-established link between rhetoric and self-representation, that chapter 4 locates Isocrates' unique contribution to the tradition of rhetoric. The sophistic tradition of eloquence and the philosophical tradition of practical wisdom come together in Isocrates' conception of public deliberation as deliberation about the good and the possible. The form proper to such a practice is a type of epideictic rhetoric that, attempted in the *Evagoras* and the *Helen* but perfected in the *Panegyricus*, blends encomiastic praise with political advice. The forum proper to this uniquely Isocratean rhetorical form is the agora, a place traditionally hospitable to intellectual exchanges but now reconstituted by Isocrates as the space where the orator's art may be displayed and the orator's political advice may be publicly disseminated.

There follows an examination of the *Panegyricus*, Isocrates' most important work, as a case in point, an instance of public deliberation, a display of eloquence and a demonstration of practical knowledge. Bringing together some of the issues covered in earlier chapters, chapter 5 takes a look at the *Panegyricus* as a rhetorical enactment of the inquiry into the good and the possible. The work exhibits the process of making ethical judgments and political choices by generating an interplay between the general case and the particular instance, the familiar past and the indeterminate present. At the same time, it displays not only oratorical eloquence but also the orator's experience, by bringing to the deliberating situation a judgment seasoned through personal and social commitments, reasoned and passionate responses, calculation and desire. Additionally, the *Panegyricus* displays the dynamics of public deliberation by enacting on the very texture of its form the deliberating process, i.e., by performing aesthetically the process of making prudent choices about the good and the possible.

Finally, in chapter 6, I examine Isocrates' claim concerning the teachability of the art of public deliberation by consulting his educational treatises, *Antidosis* and *Against the Sophists*. What emerges from the pedagogical discussions in these treatises is a theory of pedagogy that links the art of rhetoric to the polis and that promotes the instruction of rhetoric as required study for any form of active participation and involvement in political life. Because inextricably linked to the polis, Isocrates' version of rhetorical education encourages nonformalistic approaches to learning, values knowledge on the basis of its potential uses rather than for its own sake, and assesses professional educators on the basis of their contributions to the quality of democratic life in the polis rather than on the basis of their technical expertise. Rhetorical education emerges as the field of study that organizes other areas of knowledge under the common task of sustaining those structures of sociopolitical relations in the polis which safeguard citizens' freedom to pursue their interests and desires. In Isocrates' rhetorical education, the modern reader is certain to recognize important elements of an approach to learning that today goes by the name of "cultural studies." The call issued by this novel paradigm of learning, i.e., to make fields of knowledge culture-specific and socially pertinent, finds an answer in Isocrates and his lifelong effort to make rhetorical education an apprenticeship to political life.

Chapter One

Rhetoric and Social Cohesion
The "Hymn to Logos"

Despite his renown as a teacher of rhetoric, Isocrates wrote only two treatises on rhetorical education and nothing about rhetorical theory. Some scholars believe that he eventually did compose a theoretical treatise on rhetoric, which conveyed his approach to and theory of the art and which was subsequently lost.[1] But one cannot help wondering why, if he had really been preoccupied with theorizing the art of rhetoric, his theoretical preoccupation did not also surface elsewhere, in some other parts of his extant writings. He avoids using the term *rhetoric* in reference to his profession and goes so far as to label his educational program "instruction in philosophy." There will be occasion later to address his choice of this label in greater detail. For now, this work will simply acknowledge his hesitation to identify himself as a teacher of rhetoric and point out in his defense the kind of baggage that such an identity carried at the time. Indeed, various accounts by prominent intellectuals, beginning with the end of the fifth century and continuing on to Isocrates' time, concur in portraying the profession of a rhetoric teacher as popular, profitable, and fraudulent.[2] It seems that with some training in verbal quibbles, a good grip on paradoxical argumentation, and an overall dexterity in language use, one was sufficiently equipped to call himself a "sophist," take up the profession of teaching the art of rhetoric, and look for wealthy clients.[3] Within such a climate, it is understandable why Isocrates would have wanted to teach rhetoric without using the term, to continue the rhetorical education of the older Sophists without associating himself with their activities, and to advance a conception of rhetoric without formulating it explicitly.

The closest he ever comes to theorizing rhetoric is in a section of the *Nicocles*, an oration he composed for the Cyprian ruler and his student. The section has been quoted often and has come to be known, independently of its context, as Isocrates' "hymn to logos." In it Isocrates makes two principal claims about the rhetorical logos. First, logos is an instrument of devising or making. Second, as maker, logos has the potential to create strong ties among members of a society. These two claims will be examined separately in an integrated effort to show that Isocrates did hold, without articulating explicitly, a general conception of rhetoric as speech leading to concerted action for the benefit of the polis; for it is this conception of rhetoric that informed Isocrates' teaching of the art and that distinguished him from other rhetoricians. His idiosyncracy as a practicing rhetorician and teacher of rhetoric lies in the unique perspective he advanced on rhetoric as the art of speaking for the polis.

I

According to Werner Jaeger, the exaltation of logos as the "creatrix of culture and human society" reveals Isocrates' intention to give rhetoric a new mission: to employ rhetoric for the purpose of offering resolutions to political and ethical irresolutions. But the new mission assigned to rhetoric would not have been taken seriously by other intellectuals unless it was also accompanied by some effort to rearticulate earlier conceptions of persuasion. Isocrates needed to show, Jaeger goes on, that there was more to rhetoric than what Plato had made of it in the *Gorgias,* more than "a purely formal technique of hypnotizing the ignorant masses with persuasive talk" (90). The hymn to logos demonstrates, for Jaeger, Isocrates' successful rerouting of rhetoric away from the production of effects and toward the sustenance of common valuations in the polis: "For logos means speech, in the sense of rational speech and communication, which always rests ultimately upon the acknowledgment of common values" (91). While Jaeger's conclusion, that Isocrates' success was due to the ethical and political content he gave rhetoric, is warranted, his brief discussion of the hymn to logos does not answer questions regarding the altered character of rhetoric, the changes rhetoric must undergo when it enters the world of politics and ethics. More than celebrating rhetoric's influence on civilization and culture, the hymn to logos also points to a new conception of rhetoric, which this chapter will attempt to articulate.

Specifically, the discussion that follows examines the hymn to logos as an effort on Isocrates' part to give rhetoric cultural legitimacy by making logos the protagonist of traditional narratives about the origin of civilization; to associate rhetoric with civilized life by discussing logos as maker; and to link rhetoric with the production and sustenance of social bonds and communal ties by characterizing logos as guide. When taken together, these specific roles and brief characterizations of logos contribute to a conception of rhetoric that constitutes human beings as deliberating agents, that takes deliberation to be a collective enterprise, and that approaches deliberation as a collective inquiry into ethical and political choices.

The hymn begins with an exaltation of logos as the origin and cause of civilized life. Since it will be examined closely, it is included below in its entirety.

For in the other powers which we possess we are in no respect superior to other living creatures; nay, we are inferior to many in swiftness and in strength and in other resources; but, because there has been implanted in us the power to persuade each other and to make clear to each other whatever we desire, not only we have escaped the life of wild beasts, but we have come together and founded cities and made laws and invented arts; and, generally speaking, there is no institution devised by man which the power of speech has not helped us to establish. For this it is which has laid down laws concerning things just and unjust, and things base and honourable; and if it were not for these ordinances we should not be able to live with one another. It is by this also that we confute the bad and extol the good. Through this we educate the ignorant and appraise the wise; for the power to speak well is taken as the surest index of a sound understanding, and discourse which is true and lawful and just is the outward image of a good and faithful soul. With this faculty we both contend against others on matters which are open to dispute and seek light for ourselves on things which are unknown; for the same arguments which we use in persuading others when we speak in public, we employ also when we deliberate in our own thoughts; and while we call eloquent those who are able to speak before a crowd, we regard as sage those who most skilfully debate their problems in their own minds. And, if there is need to speak in brief summary of this power, we shall find that none of the things which are done with intelligence take place without the help of speech, but that in all our actions as well as in all our thoughts speech is our guide, and is most employed by those who have the most wisdom. Therefore, those who dare to speak with disrespect of educators and teachers of philosophy deserve our opprobrium no less than those who profane the sanctuaries of the gods. (*Nicocles* 5–9)

The hymn follows a typical narrative line of human history as progress and singles out human speech as the principal cause of changing human existence from an animal-like subsistence to a dignified life in society.

The portrayal of speech as the faculty most responsible for altering the course of human history from isolated to communal life is not new.[4] It finds apt expression in the mythical tradition, according to which Prometheus was said to have stolen fire and the practical arts (including speech) from the gods and to have given them to humans. In time, the myth points out, human beings were able to subjugate these divine gifts to their practical intelligence and, eventually, to turn their inarticulate cries into meaningful communication. As a result, they came together and created cities—an event that marked the beginning of life in communities and the start of civilization. Isocrates' opening passage in the hymn to logos, with its sustained comparison of humans to animals (5–6), is a direct reference to the myth of Prometheus. Already at the opening of the hymn, Isocrates places human speech at the intersection of a multiple shift: from deficiency to self-sufficiency, from isolated to communal life, and from scattered to organized forms of existence.

As has already been mentioned, these themes had been advanced by the mythical tradition; in addition, they had been reiterated by intellectuals preceding Isocrates.[5] One generation before him, Protagoras (we know from Plato) had made these themes popular once again through a detailed recounting of Prometheus' story. According to Protagoras' account of human progress, after the gods had created life on earth, they put Epimetheus and Prometheus in charge of dealing out various skills and abilities to all living creatures, so as to equip them with the means for survival on an equalizing principle. But Epimetheus squandered the goods carelessly and came to humans without any skills left. As a result, when Prometheus arrived to inspect the overall distribution of skills, he found humans, "naked, unshod, unbedded, unarmed" (*Protagoras* 321c). Wanting to equalize humans' chances for survival with other animals, but having no skills to give them, Prometheus "stole from Hephaestus and Athena wisdom in the arts together with fire . . . and he handed it there and then as a gift to man" (321d). It was these gifts, the story goes on, that eventually enabled humans "to articulate speech and words, and to invent dwellings, clothes, sandals, beds, and the foods that are of the earth" (322a).

In Protagoras' account human speech is part and parcel of the practical arts that have contributed to the survival of humankind. A similar account is given by Aeschylus, who emphasizes in *Prometheus* the intolerable hardships humans had to endure prior to possessing practical skills (442–68, 478–506). Spoken by Prometheus, the long section depicting life without thought or speech, houses or agriculture, medicine or precious metals, fire or numbers appropriately ends with this line: "Hear the sum of the whole matter in the compass of one brief word—every art possessed by man comes from Prometheus" (505–6). Dwelling on the other side of the same theme, Sophocles has the chorus in *Antigone* exalt human existence and the quality of life created by means of the practical arts: "He has learned speech and soaring thoughts and law-abiding ways in cities, and refuge from the tempestuous arrows of inhospitable frosts in the open air. Inventive always, never does he meet the future unprepared."[6]

In the hymn to logos Isocrates acknowledges the practical benefits of speech that tradition had already conferred on it. His quick comparison of humans to animals in the passage already quoted upholds the traditional perspective on speech as a faculty that, ever since the beginning of time, has helped people overcome the physical obstacles of the world in their everyday existence. Like his predecessors, Isocrates praises logos for having helped people secure for themselves the basics of survival and for having given human beings some control over their world. By representing the real, logos makes the real more manageable and the constraints imposed on living by the real more tolerable.[7] But, unlike his predecessors, Isocrates is far more interested in the relation of speech to civilized life; and the weight of his account of human survival falls, as another look at that passage makes clear, on organized life in societies: "because there has been implanted in us the power to persuade each other and to make clear to each other whatever we desire, not only we have escaped the life of wild beasts, but we have come together and founded cities and made laws and invented arts" (6).

Now the link between human speech and organized social life is a link that traditional accounts neither announce nor dispute. Even though the event of people coming together and forming cities is typically ascribed to speech, it remains unclear as to whether tradition credits speech with having merely gathered people together or with having actually caused civilized life and its most significant project, the formation of cities. Aeschylus emphasizes only the pragmatic benefits of the practical arts. Sophocles mentions "law-abiding ways in cities" as part of the human drive toward civilized life but does not make clear whether laws are to be regarded as a direct consequence of speech. Similarly, Euripides stresses the shift from confusion to order without clarifying the exact role that speech might have played in bringing about this shift: "Praise to the God who shaped in order's mould / Our lives redeemed from chaos and the brute, / First, by implanting reason, giving them / The tongue, word-herald, to interpret speech."[8] Clearly, these narratives of human progress are spacious enough to allow for the intervention of time and experience, and to account for the gradual evolution of human progress.[9] Isocrates acknowledges elsewhere the role that time and experience must have played in the long process that eventually led to civilized life: "those who first appeared upon the earth did not at the outset find the kind of life which we enjoy today, but ... procured it little by little through their own joint efforts" (*Panegyricus* 32). Yet his praise of logos in the hymn as the primary cause of the founding of cities, creation of laws, and invention of the arts links speech directly to civilized life. There is sufficient ground here to suppose that Isocrates taps on traditional accounts not only to reaffirm logos' capacity as maker, but also to extend the reach of that capacity so as to bring under its sweep organized forms of social life as well. As will be shown, Isocrates seeks to invoke tradition in order to firm up the connection between logos and civilized life, which had thus far remained undetermined. His hymn to logos seeks to establish the potential to civilize as part of the broader capacity of logos to act as a maker.

And this supposition is bound to be confirmed through a closer look at Protagoras' account of human progress, noting there the great amount of effort exerted to take the argument in the opposite direction—to dissociate speech from any relation to organized forms of social existence. Indeed, even as Protagoras' account concurs with tradition in representing logos as the force that brings people together, the same account depletes logos of its civilizing potential, for the first event of civilized life, the founding of cities, is represented by Protagoras' account as a consequence of a primitive rather than a social need. Cities are founded out of an instinct to survive, not a wish or desire to form communal life. By making use of the gifts they had inherited from Prometheus, the story goes, human beings were eventually able "to band themselves together and secure their lives by founding cities" (*Protagoras* 322b). Yet, the narrative quickly adds, even as humans had acquired technical sagacity from Prometheus, they still lacked knowledge of the political art. As a result, even as they gathered together in cities, they failed to live in them as members of a community. The narrative continues: "Now as often as they were banded together they did wrong to one another through the lack of civic art, and thus they began to be scattered again and to perish. So Zeus, fearing that our race was in danger of utter destruction, sent Hermes to bring respect (*aido*) and right (*dike*) among men, to the end that there should be regulation of cities and friendly ties to draw them together" (322b–c). Clearly, Protagoras' account relegates speech to the domain of the practical arts and consigns logos' power to bring people together to a prepolitical stage of history. According to Protagoras, it is respect and justice (*aido kai dike*), not speech, that accounts for the origin of civilized life.

The complication is, of course, that the narrative above is in fact Plato's rendition of Protagoras' account. A further complication is that Plato's rendition of Protagoras' Great Speech is part of the *Protagoras*, a work devoted to proving the claim that political virtue cannot be taught. Indeed, the dialogue goes on past the myth to expose Protagoras' failure to defend his initial boast to Socrates that he could in fact teach the political art and make Athenians good citizens (319a). Finally, there is not enough evidence to ascertain one way or another whether Plato's rendition is accurate. To say this is not to accuse Plato of having given us a false representation of Protagoras' position. Scholars have long recognized Plato's fairness in representing his opponents, his love of making the contests he enters tough for himself, and his habit of bringing willingly into the debate the most tenacious arguments of his opponents. Even so, there is always somewhere in the dialogues a so-called "crucial concession" made by Socrates' interlocutors. The question facing us then, does not so much concern Plato's faithful or inaccurate portrayal of Protagoras as it concerns the exact place in which Protagoras makes a crucial concession. Is it possible that Protagoras concedes to Socrates in the very process of narrating the myth?

W. K. C. Guthrie is troubled by the last section of Protagoras' myth. He cannot see how the same person who had once declared the infamous words "concerning the gods I cannot know either that they exist or they do not exist . . ." would have wished to make Zeus the source of human respect and justice. Still, Guthrie dispels his doubt as quickly as he expresses it. "Plato knew well," Guthrie reasons, "that Protagoras was a religious agnostic (cf. *Theaet.* 162d), and had no wish to deceive. In fact the myth is followed by a rational explanation of the main points, from which divine agents are wholly absent" (64–65). It is more likely, Guthrie argues, that the last section of the myth is Protagoras' own, and that the figure of Zeus is used by Protagoras allegorically. Hence Guthrie's conclusion about the last section of Protagoras' myth: "Zeus's decree stands for what in the non-mythical anthropologies (and in Protagoras's mind) was the work of time, bitter experience, and necessity" (66). Unlike Guthrie, the cultural anthropologist Hans Blumenberg flatly rejects the last section of the myth as Protagoras' own, claiming outrightly that Plato's rendition has, in fact, "put in Protagoras' mouth the elements that could not possibly be derived from a Sophist's lecture."[10] In making the political arts Zeus' gift, Blumenberg argues, Plato shows that just as the virtues of citizenship cannot be stolen by Prometheus, they cannot be received through the teaching of the Sophists either. In Blumenberg's words, the composite myth remains "an example of the kind of inevitability that Plato's Socrates loves so much that what cannot be stolen cannot be bought either. Consequently, when Protagoras, in the end, does not hesitate to talk about money, he has already run afoul of his own myth. What Zeus has bestowed was shielded against the negotiability that is possessed by things" (334).

Whatever the case—whether it was Protagoras or Plato who inserted into traditional narratives of human progress the distinction between practical and political arts—the force of the distinction is crystal clear, while the intention to delimit logos' capacity with making is all too evident. The reasoning advanced by Plato's rendition of Protagoras' myth is as follows.

Speech belongs to the order of practical skills; it is, as Plato calls it, a demiurgic skill δημιουργικὴ τέχνη. Much like other practical skills—agriculture and building shelters, for example—the skill of speaking can be developed to improve the quality of life and help meet an array of basic human needs. The intelligence required for developing practical skills is innate; it is ἔντεχνος σοφία, practical intelligence or technical sagacity, the first gift bestowed to human beings by Prometheus. When developed through time, practical intelligence leads to a division of labor, which makes living more tolerable. But it cannot lead to the kind of moral advancement required for living in societies. Practical intelligence, including the skill of speech, can contribute neither to a sense of right or justice (*dike*) nor to a sense of shame or respect for others (*aido*). These concern moral virtues—justice and self-control, *dikaiosyne kai sophrosyne* (323a)—which belong to the domain of the political, not the practical. As a demiurgic skill, then, speech cannot establish the kinds of bonds requisite for turning a mere collectivity of people into a vibrant political community. Speech bears a relation to the political realm that can only be accidental. For even as speech makes possible collective life in the city, which is a precondition of the political, this collectivity, the narrative stresses, is artificial and transient: people came together and founded cities as easily as they dispersed.

It is this dissociation of speech from the political that Isocrates will expend a great deal of effort to contest through his writings. In the hymn to logos his deliberate endeavor to link speech with the political domain is evident in the manner in which he describes the first event of civilized life, the founding of cities. The term he uses to indicate the coming together of people is συνέρχεσθαι, which means coming together willingly or deliberately. This is far from ἀθροίζεσθαι, the term Plato uses twice to describe the same event (322b). Ἀθροίζεσθαι means coming together in numbers, crowding together—the complete sense of Plato's passage connoting a type of togetherness formed and sustained solely out of the basic need to seek refuge in numbers. The substitution of ἀθροίζεσθαι for συνέρχεσθαι already indicates a conscious effort on the part of Isocrates to attribute to logos a type of togetherness that is as substantive as that required to bind human beings to a political community. In his narrative logos can create a unity among people not in the artificial sense of rallying together an aggregate of individuals but in the substantive sense of forming an integrated whole.

Isocrates makes other social institutions, in addition to cities, direct consequences of the type of togetherness established through speech, consequences that get lost in the English translation, "we have come together and founded cities and made laws and invented arts." The original, *συνελθόντες πόλεις ᾠκίσαμεν καὶ νόμους ἐθέμεθα καὶ τέχνας εὕρομεν*, favors the more causal construction, "having come together, we founded cities, and made laws, and invented arts." The sentence ascribes to the event of coming together (an event already caused by logos) a sense of unity that is substantive enough to warrant subsequent acts of social unification—the establishing of additional institutions that further bind social existence. In this way the possibility of interpretation opened up by Plato, that unity formed by speech in the course of human progress is an artificial and tenuous unity, is closed off here. Isocrates reiterates the point more forcefully in the next line: "there is no institution devised by man which the power of speech (*logos*) has not helped us to establish." The predicate used for logos here is *συγκατασκευάσας*, which literally makes logos not merely a maker or an establisher, a *κατασκευάσας*, but a maker-through-unity.

For Isocrates, then, logos has the potential to effect the kind of unity that binds people together substantively and fosters the desire for stronger bonds, which can only be secured through the establishing of social institutions. This interactive process between logos and social order helps explain Isocrates' following remark: Logos "has laid down laws concerning things just and unjust, and things base and honourable; and if it were not for these ordinances we should not be able to live with one another" (7). The institution of law, itself created through logos, secures meaningful bonds by turning the desire to coexist into institutionally structured ways of life. The term *oikein*, used here to capture the sense of an institutionally sanctioned coexistence, connotes something further: a verbal variant of *oikos*, household, *oikein* also means dwelling. This promotes the sense that the institution of law does not merely secure the participants' sense of coexistence but also strengthens their feeling of belonging to their community. The social order effected by the unifying potential of logos, and secured by means of establishing laws, makes participants of society feel toward each other as coinhabitants in the same household. Recall the promise made by Zeus in Protagoras' myth, that *aido* and *dike* were meant to produce not only social regulations but also friendly ties. With this association—of logos with friendly ties—Isocrates brings the political within reach of logos' unifying potential.

II

The hymn to logos concludes with this final laudation: "in all our actions as well as in all our thoughts speech is our guide" (9). Logos is a guide (*hegemon*) in the sense that it shows the way to others, leads the way.[11] In the context of the narrative about human progress, logos' propensity to guide can be understood in terms of political deliberation. Isocrates' substitution of ἀθροίζεσθαι for συνέρχεσθαι allows us to see progress toward civilized life as the result of a deliberate effort rather than the result of happenstance. In the distant past, we are led to presume, people came together out of a shared need to determine for themselves the best course of action available; each time they deliberated, they somehow settled on courses of action that took them closer to civilized life. Along the lines of political deliberation, Isocrates' hymn to logos can be viewed as a celebration of past utterances by unknown speakers who, at key junctures of human history, argued successfully the need for audiences to organize themselves around the demands of civilized existence and advocated persuasively courses of action (the founding of cities, the instituting of laws, and so on) that would provide satisfactory responses to those needs. Obviously, the explanation of progress as a result of deliberation accords with the democratic practices of political deliberation in Isocrates' time.[12] The guiding function of logos is made intelligible against the background of oratorical practices in the assembly: logos guides people by showing the way to the best course of action available.

Yet, Plato's expulsion of the rhetorical logos from the political realm does not negate speakers' and audiences' intentions to deliberate. What it does negate is logos' claim to unification. Hence the myth's portrayal (Protagoras' myth but Plato's wording) of the original event of city founding as an instance of a unified action, which nevertheless failed to produce unification: even as people came together and united themselves under a common purpose and in pursuit of a common end, their unity did not yield substantive bonds; on the contrary, they soon dispersed and quickly returned to their former, scattered manner of existing. In the context of the narrative about human progress, therefore, Isocrates is obliged to defend the guiding capacity of logos along the lines of a potential to create lasting bonds—if he is to lend any credibility to his conception of logos as a maker of unity. Protagoras' narrative account of human progress, against which Isocrates' own account becomes intelligible and by means of which his hymn to logos becomes coherent, has shown convincingly that the making of enterprises around shared purposes and common interests is not an index of substantive bonds among people.

To explicate sufficiently Isocrates' characterization of logos as guide, then, we must do more than imagine occasional utterances of deliberative oratory throughout history that led the way to civilized life by pointing to this or that course of action and by commanding, in each case, a public following. We must also consider the larger structure from which a given deliberative utterance may draw its unifying potential and acquire its guiding force. It may well be that Isocrates' general remark—having come together (συνελθόντες), we founded cities and made laws and invented arts—steers us precisely in the direction of the structure in question.

The term συνέρχεσθαι, which has already been loosely translated as "coming together deliberately," is more specifically used by Isocrates in three senses: first, in the sense of an inquiry—coming together to look for answers to common questions (*Panathenaicus* 14, 76); second, in the sense of coming together (in a political setting, such as the assembly) to deliberate (*Nicocles* 19, *Peace* 52) or to select the best course among those proposed (*Peace* 2, 9); and third, in the sense of coming together (in a religious setting, such as a festival) to form an alliance (*Panegyricus* 146, *Panathenaicus* 81) or to exchange pledges (*Panegyricus* 43, *Helen* 40, *Trapeziticus* 19, *Against Callimachus* 45). Taken together, these three senses of συνέρχεσθαι help us understand the kind of gatherings Isocrates might have had in mind when he referred to those that resulted in the creation of cities, laws, and arts. The need to deliberate, and the occasion of gathering in order to deliberate, explains the progress toward civilized life only in part.

Another important constituent of the occasion and the drive leading to civilized life is human inquiry, the ability to look for solutions to common problems and provide answers to common questions. The hymn to logos explains this ability as follows: "With this faculty we both contend against others on matters which are open to dispute and seek light for ourselves on things which are unknown; for the same arguments which we use in persuading others when we speak in public, we employ also when we deliberate in our own thoughts; and, while we call eloquent (ῥητορικούς) those who are able to speak before a crowd, we regard as sage those who most skilfully debate (διαλεχθῶσιν) their problems in their own minds" (8). The contrasts drawn by the passage between debate and circumspection, public persuasion and private conviction, political oratory and dialectic limit the explanatory power that the practices of political deliberation have for human progress, for logos is shown here to partake both of political deliberation and philosophical reflection.

Finally, the third meaning of συνέρχεσθαι assigns to logos an additional function still, as the stress is now placed on the sense of coming together for the purpose of forming alliances, exchanging pledges, or affirming social ties. We can get a better grasp of the dynamics associated with this event of coming together when we take a brief look at another passage in which Isocrates employs the term συνέρχεσθαι in the same sense. The passage is from the *Panegyricus* and describes the Greek customs affiliated with Panhellenic festivals:

Now the founders of our great festivals are justly praised for handing down to us a custom by which, having proclaimed a truce and resolved our pending quarrels, we come together (συνελθεῖν) in one place, where, as we make our prayers and sacrifices in common, we are reminded of the kinship which exists among us and are made to feel more kindly towards each other for the future, reviving our old friendships and establishing new ties. (43)

The passage refers to the kind of intercommunal exchanges practiced among Greek city-states during Panhellenic festivals. With praying as with sacrificing, with speaking to one another as with competing against one another, participants approach the various events of the festival as an occasion to safeguard and renew common bonds or, as the passage puts it, to revive old friendships and establish new ties.

Even as Isocrates puts the rhetorical logos at center stage in his narrative about civilization, even as he relies on political deliberation to make human progression toward a certain end intelligible, he does not conflate logos with political oratory; nor does he conflate deliberation with deliberating practices in the assembly. Rather, he expands the notion of deliberation to make allowances for the capacity to carry out a sustained inquiry as well as the concern to form or preserve social ties. That such a process of deliberation does not reflect the deliberating practices in the Athenian assembly is confirmed by the generic definition Aristotle was to give later to political oratory, which as a whole emerged out of these practices, as deliberation about the means to action, not the ends. And it is this sense of orchestrating means and ends through deliberation that Isocrates' following remark conveys: "With this faculty we . . . seek light for ourselves (σκοπούμεθα) on things which are unknown" (8). Σκοπεύειν integrates the sense of considering in general with the sense of looking into something specific. Logos guided humans to progress by directing them not only to courses of action but also to inquiries about the ends such courses were meant to attain—namely, the quality of their ties as a people.

The three occasions Isocrates attaches to the event of coming together (an inquiry, a choice of action, an affirmation of common ties) indicate, then, the parameters of an integrated situation that drew people together and consolidated many individuals into one group. And since the event of coming together is itself attributed to logos (Nicocles 6), we are asked to see logos as responsible for integrating the three situations together and for prompting people to gather together and provide answers through deliberation. This enriches, as it also complicates, our understanding of the guiding capacity of logos, for we are called to see logos guiding audiences to respond to the need of selecting the best course of action among those proposed, the need to inquire into all options available (including those not yet uttered or disclosed), and the need to create new or sustain old ties. And we could not possibly integrate these various guiding functions of logos unless we were to shift the terms of the discussion and consider "guiding" not in the sense of compelling someone to act but in the sense of positioning someone toward the act about to be taken.

This latter sense is encouraged by Isocrates' narrative. The progress toward civilization is not so much punctuated by a series of discrete events in time as it is conveyed by means of a range of attitudes. The momentous episode of instituting laws, for instance, is treated not as an event to be recounted but as an attitude to be described: "[logos] has laid down laws concerning things just and unjust, and things base and honourable; and if it were not for these ordinances we should not be able to live with one another" (7). What is conveyed here is neither action nor eventfulness but rather a self-understanding, a way of conducting oneself and of relating to one another in the city. This urges us to grasp the guiding function of logos as a gesture of directing audiences to deliberate by assuming a particular self-understanding and by entering the situation of deliberation in accordance to that self-understanding.[13] Before the particular course of action is even proposed, logos guides by promoting a particular self-understanding and by eliciting audiences to understand themselves in ways that make collective participation and deliberation seem possible and desirable.[14]

Isocrates' narrative of human progress presumes, then, not only a series of collective steps that eventually led to civilized life, but also a collective self-understanding by means of which these steps could be regarded as possible and desirable. The logos he celebrates throughout his narrative is a signifier for utterances that not only successfully created exigencies around a disorderly, fragmented, and isolated existence but also successfully interpellated audiences as political agents. Along with guiding people to collective pursuits, therefore, the civilizing logos must also be seen as having additionally guided people's self-understanding as members of a collectivity consolidated by the kinds of social fabric they had themselves established or could envision themselves capable of establishing. Logos addressed audiences as participants of a collective inquiry shaped not only around the demands of taking action but also around the demands of sustaining their self-understanding as political agents. It positioned audiences within a setting where their political agency could be exercised, both in terms of their freedom to pursue the opportunities created by their consolidation into a group and in terms of their obligation to sustain the bonds of that consolidation. Finally, logos named audiences as guardians of their common welfare with regard to their capacity to make autonomous decisions and their self-understanding as makers of a social order that determined their autonomy.

Isocrates grafts the guiding capacity of logos onto the makings of a symbolic crafting that shapes the real by attributing to it exigencies that must be dealt with immediately, and he assigns auditors with political identities necessary to confront these exigencies and resolve their unbearable irresolutions.[15] In Protagoras' myth we saw a barrier being erected between speech, on the one hand, and aido and dike, on the other. All capacity to create substantive bonds, lasting associations, or enduring friendships was given over to aido and dike, while speech was credited with forming short-lived enterprises or transient pursuits. In relation to this clear-cut division, Isocrates' rhetorical project can now be understood as an effort to tinker with these boundaries and to recast the division between ephemeral and lasting bonds not as Protagoras had, as a difference between practical and political arts, but as a difference in the kind of exigencies created and the type of identities mobilized. For Isocrates, logos can create an exigency out of practical needs (sheltering, agriculture, and so on) and mobilize a pragmatic self-understanding linked to survival; but it can also create an exigency out of political needs and mobilize a political self-understanding linked to ethico-social concerns. As long as logos creates exigencies out of needs that can be filled expediently or interests that can be met enterprisingly, as long as it mobilizes an identity constructed around self-interest, the unifying potential of logos will never amount to anything more than an enterprise, a partnership, a coalition. And, as Protagoras' myth has shown, once the pressing demands of these needs, interests, or purposes are met, the ties that held together the enterprise, partnership, or coalition will dissipate. But if logos were to link an exigency to a political self-understanding—in other words, mobilize an identity constructed around social and ethical concerns—then, Isocrates was convinced, the same social cohesion the gods had once assigned to aido and dike could now be assigned to logos.

III

Earlier in this study I claimed that Isocrates' general conception of rhetoric, as speech leading to action for the benefit of the polis, can be derived from his formulation of logos as maker and guide—a formulation that partook of a larger tradition and issued a challenge to it. It might be helpful at this juncture to pause and consider a few broad remarks that would further clarify that tradition and that challenge.

Protagoras' claim that he could use logos to teach the political art and turn Athenian youth into virtuous citizens reflects a time when the Athenians, well immersed in an anthropocentric tradition, looked to speech as one more confirmation of their self-understanding as agents of their own political condition.[16] It is this link between speech and political agency that Protagoras reiterates as he promises the young Hippocrates that he will teach him to "have most influence on public affairs both in speech and in action" (*Protagoras* 319a). Along with Protagoras, other Sophists similarly regarded speech as an indication of their self-determination. Thus, Thrasymachus in *The Constitution* encourages citizens to speak against the state of affairs, investing speech with the power to alter the shape of politics at the time.[17] And Gorgias portrays speech as an instrument that, if employed skillfully, can effect the kind of impact one desires.[18] In an analogy with the potency of drugs, Gorgias invests speech in the *Helen* with extraordinary healing and poisoning effects (14), with the power to effect even the divinest of deeds (8), and with the overall potential to persuade people to feel, think, and act. It is this general sentiment about logos, its power to create a desired impact and its potential to effect the shape of human affairs, that Plato criticized.

Plato's objections to the Sophists are too numerous to list and too well known to reiterate here.[19] The general thrust of Plato's critique is that the influence with which the Sophists had invested logos was harmful to the polis. While conceding the impact that rhetoric could have, and regarding the Sophists as able to turn the known world upside down with their masterful manipulation of logos (*Phaedrus* 267a), Plato raised the following main objections. First, the rhetorical logos is more of a hindrance than an aid in discovering the true nature of things—all logos can do is manipulate appearances and create misleading perceptions. Second, the rhetorical logos serves only the interests of speakers without contributing to the moral improvement of listeners. Third, if one were to judge rhetoric by the state of political affairs at the time, one could only conclude that the practical applications of the rhetorical logos are harmful to the polis and undesirable to the citizens.

Faced with the sophistical conceptualization of logos and Plato's objection to it, Isocrates advanced a notion of logos that, borrowing from both, contributed to a unique conception of rhetoric. From the Sophists, Isocrates borrowed the notion of logos as a maker of culture, a notion that, as has already been shown, other Athenian intellectuals subscribed to as well. And he continued that strand of intellectual tradition according to which logos was regarded as an instrument humans could use to confront the constraints of the real, by interposing logos between themselves and the world. He endorsed, in other words, the common view that this interposition—whose most basic function is representation by name—afforded people with control over their world; he also supported the view that as soon as things are represented, they lose their fearful and mysterious ambience and become understandable and manageable.[20]

Isocrates sought to link this notion of logos to a conception of rhetoric that would repeat the Protagorean project, that is, teach people to control language for the purpose of advancing their private and collective interests.[21] Yet, such a repetition was, strictly speaking, impossible, for, as many scholars have long pointed out, the notion of logos as maker of culture had been taken up and used in ways entirely unanticipated by Protagoras' political project.[22] The gap separating the use of logos to make things intelligible and the conception of everything cultural as arbitrarily made was closing in rapidly.[23] Conventions and customs, but also institutions and laws, became understood as arbitrary creations, makings of an ever-pliable language and results of relative uses.[24] Gorgias linked the nonreferential capacity of language with the power to have control—this time "control" being understood not in the sense of imposing intelligence on the physical world but in the sense of imposing one's will on others, in the sense of manipulation and domination.[25]

Accepting Gorgias' nonreferential thrust of rhetoric and conceding to its potentially evil uses, yet insisting on the civic purpose Protagoras had given the art, Isocrates focused on the "citizenly" uses of rhetoric. In the hymn to logos he portrayed human progress as the outcome of people who came together determined to create a social order they would readily enter and within which they would willingly bind themselves to one another as citizens. Such a portrait relies on the nonreferential capacity Gorgias had assigned to logos in *The Nonexistent*—to create something out of nothing—as well as on the capacity Protagoras had assigned to logos—to shape individuals into citizens. At the same time, by depicting progress exclusively in terms of advances commonly beneficial to human beings, this portrait of logos leaves out Gorgias' association of logos with manipulation as well as Protagoras' connection of logos to virtuous conduct. Throughout his works Isocrates made a concerted effort to dissociate manipulative rhetoric from his educational program and to link his own version of rhetoric to a pragmatic view of virtue, a moral conduct in everyday life rather than an ethics.

Continuing some aspects of the tradition and changing others, then, Isocrates could erect a conception of rhetoric as a citizenly instrument meant to promote actions for the benefit of the polis. Such a conception of rhetoric could accept, in turn, and in fact agree with, Plato's objections to the art, for Plato's critique could now be shown to apply only to practices of oratory outside Isocrates' version, that is, only to uncitizenly uses of rhetoric. Constructing the hymn to logos around the deliberative process, Isocrates anticipated questions about the relative character of collective benefits. These were to be determined, the overall narrative toward human progress suggests, on a case-by-case basis and by means of the situational demands of collective deliberation—as long as the deliberating process involved political and ethical choices and addressed questions about the good and the possible for the polis. Isocrates' version of deliberation will be examined in chapter 5. One last remark here will conclude this brief section on Isocrates' relation to the rhetorical tradition.

Relying on the notion of logos as maker and guide, Isocrates put rhetorical education to the task of making individuals into citizens by guiding their self-understanding in the direction of citizenship. Unlike Protagoras, however, he did not look to citizenship as a normative concept; rather, he sought, in Gorgias' fashion, to construct it. To the extent that students of rhetoric would learn to understand themselves as citizens, they would never put oratory to evil use; for, by definition, they would use the art in a citizenly manner. It is Isocrates' construction of citizenship and the citizenly uses of rhetoric that we will next examine.

Chapter Two

Speaking Like a Citizen
Citizenship, Leadership, and Community in *Nicocles*

Nicocles and its companion piece *To Nicocles* constitute Isocrates' advice to a young ruler who succeeded his father to the throne of Cyprus.[1] In these orations Isocrates outlines some precepts of good leadership and advises Nicocles how to lead his people and what to expect of them. The presumption that a ruler would want to be advised on how to become a good leader, when he is already a king, may seem odd. But the turbulent world of the first part of the fourth century and the widespread revolts against tyrannies indicate otherwise.[2] The frequent democratic outbreaks throughout the Mediterranean conveyed a disquietude to remaining monarchs, a timely uneasiness that accorded with the timeless lessons of Greek history about the workings of fate: no tyrant, however powerful, can ever succeed in placing himself above the chance of a radical reversal of fortune. There are good reasons, then, why Nicocles would have wanted to hear Isocrates' advice on how to address his subjects so as to be perceived as a leader rather than as a tyrant.

This raises an interesting issue about the word of the king in relation to his sovereign rule. By speaking to his people, Nicocles presumably stood a better chance to make his throne more secure and his monarchy more stable. But if the word of the king was synonymous with the law of the land (τοὺς λόγους τοὺς ἐμοὺς νόμους εἶναι, *Nicocles* 62), what could a speech accomplish that could not be accomplished through a king's decree? Of what help could persuasion possibly be to someone with the authority to make law by merely pronouncing the all-encompassing proclamation "thou shall do as I say"? Clearly, Isocrates believed that Nicocles' logos could have a power in excess of Nicocles' decree, and he wrote this oration out of that conviction, namely, that he could show the power differential that lies between rhetorical logos and a royal decree, between a leader addressing his audience and a king summoning his subjects.

Isocrates' effort to offer advice to a ruler is not unique. It has its roots in a long tradition of orators and poets who applied their craft in the service of instructing would-be leaders or rulers already in power. Following the tradition of the Sophists, Isocrates' advice to Nicocles repeats an important rhetorical principle: that power has a discursive base and that the words of a leader are as authoritative as is the text produced. What may be uniquely Isocratean is the effort to construct textual authority around the ruler's role as citizen. Indeed, as will be shown, Nicocles' status as citizen exceeds in authority his status as king. According to the logic of the oration, his rule will be made secure and his leadership will remain uncontested so long as he learns to speak like a citizen.

But if this is the case, Isocrates' oration would pertain not merely to Nicocles but also to anyone interested in political leadership and its relation to textual authority. The instruction offered to Nicocles could make an invaluable lesson to Isocrates' students and an important part of their training in political deliberation. Even as it was written for a Cyprian king, therefore, we cannot ignore the contributions the oration stood to make to young Athenians who had come to Isocrates convinced that the rhetorical education they were about to receive would give them a better chance to become Athens' political leaders one day. For these reasons, it should be profitable to examine Isocrates' advice to Nicocles as a lesson in political deliberation, a discourse on the relationship between textual authority and political leadership. Indeed, as with other Isocratean works, *Nicocles* is not merely an oration but also a textbook,[3] a requirement in the education of students interested in learning[4] how to speak, according to Isocrates, like leaders in the polis.

I

The gist of Isocrates' advice is that political leadership must issue from the precepts of justice and temperance. Nicocles must exercise his sovereign rule in ways that accord with the law and temper his absolute power through discipline and self-control. In turn, he can expect the same of his subjects (a topic on which Isocrates further elaborates in *To Nicocles*) and demand that they conduct themselves in accordance with the law of the land and that they engage in their pursuits, relations, and various other activities with restraint and self-control. Clearly, the nature of the argument situates political conduct within social relations among citizens and addresses political leadership as an ethical enterprise. In order to establish oneself as leader, one must make oneself accountable to the laws of the state and the canons of citizenship. To be perceived as a leader, one must prove to be a good citizen first, a leader in the rules of conduct expected by and characteristic of a virtuous citizen.

This explains why Isocrates has Nicocles take his case to the Cyprian people in a narrative intended to recount publicly his past dealings and meant to demonstrate his adherence to norms of good citizenship, the virtues of justice and temperance (dikaiosyne kai sophrosyne), ever since his ascension to the throne. Throughout the narrative justice is argued in terms of deeds Nicocles performed concerning such matters as replenishing the treasury and advancing the state's prosperity, paying people back who had been robbed by various enemies, never killing or exiling anyone, and never confiscating anyone's property (31ff.). With regard to temperance, the case is made in terms of such topics as having been faithful to his wife and having restrained his absolute power with an eye to preserving harmony in his private (household) and public affairs (entire dominion) (36ff.). What Isocrates has Nicocles express through the narrative is that he has been a good king and that his rule has thus far been informed by the norms of citizenship. Clearly, Isocrates is banking on the assumption that in order to be perceived as a good king by the Cyprians, Nicocles must first establish that he is one of them. He must demonstrate that he possesses attitudes and concerns they value and that he belongs to a social order they identify with and wish to be subjected by.

The narrative of Nicocles' past conduct ends with this recapitulating remark: "When I was left by my father without means, I was so just in my dealings as to injure not one of my citizens; but when I gained the power to do whatever I pleased, I proved myself more temperate than men in private station" (45). Oddly enough, the criteria for assessing a king's actions, as well as for testing his claim to good leadership, turn out to be provided by ordinary, unwritten codes of civility among members of a society. Nicocles deserves to be thought of as a good king and merits the title of a good leader, the argument goes, because in his dealings with other citizens he has conducted himself as a just and tempered citizen would have been expected to. The narrative of Nicocles' past deeds, which was supposed to give an account of his behavior and demonstrate the excellence of his rule, shifts registers from leadership to citizenship, and the events narrated end up demonstrating the just and tempered nature of his conduct as citizen rather than as ruler. The nature of the argument and the content of the narrative also show what it means to have Nicocles assume the position of a leader. Such positioning entails nothing more than taking up and assuming the perspective of a citizen: to address the people of Cyprus as their leader rather than as their ruler, Nicocles must speak to them as a citizen speaking to other citizens.

A question raised earlier—how is it that Nicocles' logos may have a power in excess of his decree?—has opened the way in the direction not of excess but of rudiments. To make his throne more secure, the logic of the narrative goes, Nicocles must relinquish the authority of a king and assume the perspective of a leader; yet this requires nothing more than taking up the position of an ordinary member of the state and speaking as a citizen. The moves performed by the oration indicate not the operations of excess but the opposite operations of doing away with all excess in an effort to get to some core. On its way to giving Nicocles more authority than he commands as king, the oration moves forward by gradually stripping him of all rank and social status, down to the very core—his status as ordinary citizen. For it is Nicocles as *polites* who will finally be shown to command power and the words he speaks as citizen that will ultimately emerge as the locus of the greatest political authority.

The textual operations of the oration bring us in contact with one of the democratic veins traversing the text. The process of constructing citizenship as the locus of authority sheds light on the structural equality that exists—albeit as a potential—in the democratic polis between ordinary citizens and aristocrats. No amount of political power one enjoys due to social status can ever be, the text underscores, inherently superior to the authority an ordinary Athenian citizen can potentially command. No claim to nobility of birth can ever act as a substitute to logos. The democratizing effect of education, an effect whose traces determine the operations of the narrative, undoes the hierarchical binaries king/citizen, decree/persuasion, blood/logos with which the oration began. Consequently, students of Isocrates, undoubtedly close readers of this oration, could draw away the following lesson about rhetoric: because the authority of a given discourse lies in the audience's attitude toward the speaker, it is the quality of the speaker's rhetorical education that is the principal factor here, not the quantity of the speaker's wealth, his rank or social status. It is the force of this lesson that must have led Isocrates to boast about the authority of an ordinary citizen's words as he spoke to Philip. "And do not be surprised," he says to the Macedonian king, "that I, who am not a general nor a public orator nor in any other position of authority, have expressed myself to you more boldly than the others" (*To Philip* 81).

The term *democratic vein* is used in the above paragraph rather than *democratic logic* because not everything in *Nicocles* can be regarded as democratic. Indeed the oration can also be interpreted as a text well suited to carry out a ruler's desire to elicit compliance from his subjects and appropriate to this monarch's specific wishes to shape Cyprian citizens into obedient servants. It is this line of interpretation that Norman Baynes has chosen to follow in reading *Nicocles* as "surely one of the strangest writings produced under the Athenian democracy by anyone who claimed to be a leader of political opinion" (149). For Baynes, the oration provides a defense of monarchy as the best form of constitution and offers a justification of tyranny in the eloquent portrait of the monarch's character, the *arete* of Nicocles. In his words, the entire oration is reducible to a "laudation of a 'totalitarian' State" (151).

Exaggerated though it may be, Baynes' conclusion follows a line of interpretation that finds ample support in Isocrates' personal politics and, consequently, cannot be dismissed outrightly. Isocrates' call for a more restricted form of democracy in the *Areopagiticus*, his condemnation of the democratic practice to appoint public officials through a lottery system in the *Peace*, and, most important, his ongoing campaign for a strong leader in Athens, which eventually led to his enthusiastic support of a non-Athenian for that post (the Macedonian Philip)—these political sentiments pose interpretative difficulties to anyone wishing to link Isocratean thought with a democratic politics. My own approach to this difficulty is to maintain a distinction between Isocrates' personal politics and his larger effort to politicize the art of rhetoric. Once this distinction is maintained, once we see the political as the ground of various politics, then Isocrates' oligarchic sympathies can be regarded as an idiosyncratic preference, the personal implementation of a structure whose constituent principles neither necessitate this particular implementation nor compel that particular politics. That Isocrates himself chose to implement his own thought in a specific manner does not mean that his thought needs to be interpreted similarly by us or by his contemporaries. Nor should we presume to suppose that Isocrates' politics were consistently aligned with the oligarchic party. The party lines in Classical Athens were never precise, and the divide between democrats and oligarchs was much more flexible than people have come to be accustomed to in modern times. The political in Isocrates is traversed simultaneously by a number of oligarchic as well as democratic strands.

And it is this rich texture of Isocrates' political thought that permits Jaeger to recognize in *Nicocles* a strand in praise of monarchy and, at the same time, to caution against an interpretation of the oration as a laudation of tyranny. According to Jaeger, Isocrates "does more than accept tyranny as a given fact in power-politics." He additionally draws on historical examples to show that states which had benefited from monarchy were also the states governed by good leaders. In Jaeger's words, "Isocrates does not attempt to limit the tyrant's power by written laws or constitutions. His subjects are expressly directed to consider his word as their law. Nothing restrains him except the virtues of justice and self-control. These—not the warlike qualities usually ascribed to great monarchs— are the qualities which Nicocles describes as the pillars of his rule" (87). Unlike Baynes, who saw Isocrates defending monarchy for Athenian politics under the pretext of praising a monarch away from Athens, Jaeger regards Isocrates as participating in the political spirit of his times and as contributing to the larger effort of the times "to transform tyranny into 'a gentler constitution'" (87). Of the two, it is Jaeger's reading that coheres with Isocrates' own remarks about *Nicocles* as an oration aimed at advising a tyrant to be a good leader, a representative of his people: "I have expressed myself to Nicocles as a free man and an Athenian should, not paying court to his wealth nor to his power, but pleading the cause of his subjects, and striving with all my powers to secure for them the mildest government possible. And since in addressing a king I have spoken for his subjects, surely I would urge upon men who live under a democracy to pay court to the people" (*Antidosis* 70).

Whatever Isocrates' particular politics might have been behind his portrayal of Nicocles as an ideal leader, the political principle informing such a portrait—a conduct guided by dike and aido—names the condition that must be met if a person may turn from an individual into a social being and a number of persons may turn from an aggregate of individuals into a society. Dike and aido, as we saw in the *Protagoras*, are the twin forces that supply the type of cohesion necessary for creating lasting bonds among individuals gathered together, the two agents that transform a transient collectivity into a polis. Following *Protagoras*, the narrative in *Nicocles* enacts a drama whose major protagonists, dike and aido, come in contact with a king and shape him into a citizen.

This explains the stress Isocrates placed on the narrative of Nicocles' past, a narrative meant to demonstrate that his rise to the throne was a direct consequence of his conduct as a citizen. Through the narrative Nicocles does not merely emerge as a citizen bound to the same laws and codes of civil propriety as any other ordinary citizen; he in fact emerges as the best citizen. Indeed, Isocrates places Nicocles in competition with other citizens and situates him in a rivalry among other equals, each one vying, as it were, for the prize of the best citizen. It is not enough, it appears, that Nicocles pass the test of the good citizen in the eyes of his subjects; he must also show that he has passed the test with flying colors. That he has proved himself to be "more tempered than men in private station" is a remark that bespeaks not only of his willingness to be judged as an ordinary citizen but also of his confidence that, if that judgment were to be made on comparative grounds, he would have emerged as the best citizen. This is made more evident yet by the following statement: "I conceived, therefore, that the noblest thing that I could do was to be able to excel my fellows in those virtues [justice and temperance] in which the bad have no share, and which are the truest and the most abiding and deserve the greatest praise" (43). Clearly, Isocrates casts the power of the king as emanating directly from the authority he has earned through his contributions to the political order of his state. His personal gain and social advance to kingship are the direct results of his political excellence, his conduct as polites. Once Nicocles' throne is perceived as the result not of birth but of merit, then, his position as leader of his people will be perceived as a natural extension of his credentials as a leading citizen, which, in turn, will secure his rule.

In structuring citizenship as a construct that maintains a continuous relationship between politics and ethics, Isocrates follows the sophistic tradition and especially Protagoras. For, of all the Sophists, it was Protagoras who put a premium on citizenship and who, in fact, framed his entire program in rhetoric as education of the citizen. Indeed Protagoras stated his educational objective as the specific aim "to make men good citizens, ποιεῖν ἄνδρας ἀγαθοὺς πολίτας" (*Protagoras* 319a). With Protagoras, citizenship was discussed as a process of indoctrination and enculturation, both a voluntary and an involuntary process.[5] Thus, in the case of the individual as a child Protagoras invokes an array of forces that combine to shape the child into something the youngster does not want to become. "They teach and admonish them from earliest childhood till the last day of their lives. As soon as one of them grasps what is said to him, the nurse, the mother, the tutor, and the father himself strive hard that the child may excel, and as each act and word occurs they teach and impress upon him that this is just, and that unjust, one thing noble, another base, one holy, another unholy, and that he is to do this, and not do that. If he readily obeys,—so; but if not, they treat him as a bent and twisted piece of wood and straighten him with threats and blows" (325c–d). As the child grows older, threats are supplemented with admonitions and praises, and the entrance into good citizenship is now based mostly on persuasive appeals: "here they meet with many admonitions, many descriptions and praises and eulogies of good men in times past, that the boy in envy may imitate them and yearn to become even as they" (325e–326a). Finally, even after an individual becomes a competent citizen, the process of indoctrination still continues, since there are always those who excel "ever so little in showing the way to virtue" (328a). Protagoras proclaims himself to be one such instance of excellence: "Such an one I take myself to be, excelling all other men in the gift of assisting people to become good and true, and giving full value for the fee that I charge" (328b).

Protagoras' account of the socializing process is informed by the notion of citizenship as a type of political participation that is constitutive of a fully human life and inextricably connected with human well-being. There is no distinction assumed here between an individual and a polites, for it is through political participation that one realizes one's capacity both as an autonomous agent and as a complete person. Political excellence and personal excellence are the products of the same process and the results of one's contributions to a common project, the survival and flourishing of the community. Being a citizen, therefore, affords one the possibility to attain, at one and the same time, a personal and a political excellence. And those who attain this excellence are the leaders of the community.

Yet this democratic ideal—seen from an outsider's point of view as realizable by the Athenians of the fifth century—had turned out to be unrealizable. By Isocrates' time it had become evident that the everyday practices of the Athenians had evolved in a direction other than the one Protagoras had presumed to be possible. Indeed, the Athenians of the fourth century inherited a history of practices that disconfirmed the unification of the individual and the political in the polites. One after another, political leaders following Pericles had advocated policies out of a personal motivation. Military leaders had undertaken expeditions with an eye to advancing their own status in the polis. And administrative officials had used public offices to promote their own individual prosperity at the cost of the public treasury. These instances gave historical force to the widespread feeling among the Athenians of Isocrates' day—that the individual did not partake of the collective and that socio-economic advancement did not coincide with political excellence.

The radically different circumstances Isocrates faced explain his distinct approach to citizenship. The gap in the Athenians' self-understanding between individuals and *politai* could no longer be resolved by him in the manner Protagoras had offered to resolve it. The experiment with democracy had by now created a long history of practices that offered resilience to the possibility of realizing some of the democratic ideals that had once been seen as realizable. The dilemma facing Isocrates was not an intellectual one—how to bridge the gap between the individual and the collective. Rather it was a pragmatic one—how to show that being a good citizen was not merely an intrinsic good but could still on many occasions lead to socio-economic success. The road to socio-economic success, Isocrates sought to demonstrate, did not have to be paved with noncitizenly conduct.

Unlike Protagoras, Isocrates does not cast his instruction as one more mechanism of social indoctrination or enculturation aiming to shape individuals into citizens.[6] Rather he deals with the difficulties that emerge following the processes of indoctrinating the youth, past the mechanisms and apparatuses of enculturation, at the moment when the public recognizes or suspects a disjuncture between a prominent person's words and the public's collective understanding of what a citizen's conduct ought to be.[7] With Isocrates, citizenship is attached instead to a process of recuperation. For him, citizenship is an identity that must be reclaimed, and the problem with citizenship appears to be how to disclose that identity pub-

licly—how a king can prove that his royal status did not violate but actually derived from his status as citizen, or how an orator can demonstrate
that his words did not originate in his interest for self-advantage but in his
position as the citizen who speaks as a member of the polis.

Underlying Isocrates' insistence on recuperating the position of citizenship (for Nicocles, when he addressed the Cyprians; for himself, when he
addressed Philip; and for his students, when they sought to learn how
to address the Athenians) there appears to be a democratic valorization
of the political identity commonly understood as "the citizen." Isocrates
took that valorization as a given and sought to teach his students to speak
in line with their identity as citizens, recognizing well that this particular
identity still acted in his society as a regulating mechanism of all other social roles; that wealth, power, and speech were legitimate or illegitimate
depending on whether or not they issued from that identity; and that they
were encoded as acceptable or unacceptable pursuits, glorious or tyrannical ventures, honorable or dishonorable ends solely on the basis of that
identity. Isocrates' effort to recuperate citizenship, in other words, is also
an effort to reclaim the equality associated with citizenship and to valorize political equality above socio-economic inequality. Even at a time
when socio-economic inequalities dominated the relations of Athenians,
the polis must still be regarded, he is saying, as the source of all human
excellence, political as well as social.

At the end of the first chapter political identity was discussed as a symbolic crafting, a discursively constructed site, an ethico-political space
opened by logos. The potential of logos to unify was shown to rest on its
capacity to guide people to that space wherein they could understand
themselves as members not only of a collectivity or a gathering but of an
integrated whole—as citizens of a community held together by substantive bonds. And now, in the context of *Nicocles*, we see Isocrates guiding
the king/orator to that same place and positioning Nicocles across his audience by constructing his identity as that of a citizen. To unify audiences,
we learn from *Nicocles*, it is not enough that logos interpellate individuals
as citizens; logos must also emanate from the same space it seeks to guide
others in. Most important, logos must be perceived by audiences as an assertion of the speaker's political identity rather than the speaker's socio-
economic status. Yet this obliged Isocrates to set up boundaries around
that space and to divide conduct in terms of what falls within or outside
the parameters of one's identity as citizen. And it is this effort to set up
boundaries and map out the inside and outside of a citizen's identity that
must next be documented if we are to understand at all what it means, according to Isocrates, to speak as a citizen and why speaking as a citizen is
a precondition to political leadership.

II

Isocrates situates Nicocles in the position of citizen because, as we have seen, wealth, status, and oratory, though not evil in themselves, are nevertheless suspect. The possibility always exists that the economic prosperity, social prestige, or oratorical fame one enjoys at present might have been attained through unjust or immoderate ways. Occupying the position of a citizen entails, by definition, one's submission to the principle that others must be treated in a just and moderate fashion, in other words, in accordance to the virtues of justice and temperance (dikaiosyne and sophrosyne). This means that status, wealth, and oratory are indexes of excellence of character when they are the direct outcomes or the consequences of one's just and tempered conduct, but indicative of a distorted character if they are attained through any means that violate or stretch the bounds of justice and temperance. This, we saw, was the purpose behind the narrative account of Nicocles' past deeds—to demonstrate to his audience that his past conduct in relation to other citizens fell within the ethical boundaries of the just and the moderate, and that the authority of his word and office were in fact the direct results of a conduct fitting to a model citizen.

Dikaiosyne and sophrosyne do not merely determine the horizon of an agent's moral conduct.[8] Because they circumscribe political identities, they also implicate the conduct of the entire polis.[9] The moral and political behavior of the city, as we saw in *Protagoras*, does not merely rest on the citizen body; it additionally rests on the assumption that any citizen has something of value to contribute to moral and political questions concerning public affairs. As Protagoras puts it to Socrates, "your fellow-citizens have good reason for admitting a smith's or cobbler's counsel in public affairs" (324c). In deciding to undertake a particular expedition or to assume a particular conduct toward its allies, the city, in effect, patterns its behavior after the words of its citizens.[10] If the advice offered is spoken with words out of a citizenly character, or outside the bounds of justice and temperance circumscribing a citizen's conduct, then the city will assume a noncitizenly behavior toward its allies and, as a result, risk its own welfare. As does a citizen's standing in the polis, so does the city's reputation rest on whether or not the power it commands and the wealth it enjoys are legitimate outcomes or wrongful transgressions of a normative conduct, i.e., a just and tempered treatment of others.

Given this link between the conduct of the citizen and the behavior of the city, and given that citizens' words determine the city's conduct, it should not be surprising to see Isocrates time and again invoke dikaiosyne and sophrosyne as criteria for assessing oratory. Public orators and politicians (positions which, incidentally, amounted to one and the same thing in Classical Athens) exerted a great deal of influence on shaping public opinion in the assembly, while logographers specializing in court oratory had the ability to affect the verdicts of the jury.[11] This gave oratory an especially crucial function in the polis; for in following the citizens' directive to interpret the law or implement legislative measures, the city inadvertently carried out the wishes of the most persuasive orators.[12] And since oratory played such an important role in determining the city's conduct—among its own citizens as well as toward other cities—it ought to be subjected, as far as Isocrates was concerned, to the same standards of conduct that citizens and polity alike were expected to uphold.

Isocrates' attention to conduct at multiple registers (the moral, the political, the socio-economic, the oratorical) prevents us from understanding dikaiosyne and sophrosyne solely as virtues governing individual behavior. Nor should we take Isocrates' frequent discussions of dikaiosyne and sophrosyne as merely intended to demarcate the boundaries of a citizen's moral identity. Rather we should keep an eye out for potential intersections between registers and attend to the possibility that what may strike us as discourse on morality or foreign policy may often turn out to be an invaluable guide to our understanding of Isocrates' attitude toward oratorical practices in his day. For, as will be shown, the lines Isocrates draws to arrange conduct (of the citizen or the city) into such oppositions as honest/dishonest, ethical/unethical, honorable/dishonorable are the same lines he draws to divide oratorical practices into identical sets of oppositions.

We may begin to investigate these possibilities by focusing on a general remark Isocrates makes about human nature. The remark appears in the *Antidosis* as a response to his own brief inquiry into the human propensity to err. To the question "what are the objects which make people venture to do evil?" he provides this response: "I maintain that everyone does everything which he does for the sake of pleasure or gain or honour (ἡδονῆς ἢ κέρδους ἢ τιμῆς); for I observe that no desire springs up in men save for these objects" (217). Human motivation provides for Isocrates a convenient grid onto which he may graft citizenly conduct and map out the workings of desire.

To determine what bearing the desire for pleasure or gain may have on one's treatment of fellow citizens, we must first look at the impact of desire upon the self. Isocrates follows Plato in using metaphors of eating to link the pleasurable with the harmful:[13] "the majority take pleasure in the foods and habits which injure both the body and the soul" (*Peace* 109). In turn, he relies on that same linkage to align the desire for pleasure in sharp contrast to self-interest. As he says to Nicocles, "the majority of men do not take pleasure in the food that is the most wholesome . . . hav[ing] tastes which are in every way contrary to their best interests" (*To Nicocles* 45). Thus, unlike Plato, who placed the desire for pleasure, along with the care for one's worldly interests, in opposition to the soul, Isocrates placed the desire for pleasure in opposition to the pursuit of self-interests. As he puts it, "many men, because of their incontinence, are not amenable to reason, but neglect their true interests and rush on in the pursuit of pleasure" (ἀμελήσαντες τοῦ συμφέροντος ἐπὶ τὰς ἡδονὰς ὁρμῶσιν) (*Antidosis* 221).

The opposition of self-interest to pleasure and gain is grafted by Isocrates onto the spatial configuration of an inside/outside polarity. Household signifies the site of one's affairs and self-interests, while the space outside the household designates the source of potential pleasure and gain for the self as well as the site of possessions belonging to other people. To the extent that pleasure or gain is often obtained at others' expense, causing undue pain to other people (*Nicocles* 40) or injury to fellow citizens (*To Timotheus* 4), the desire for immodest pleasure and illegitimate gain falls outside the domain of a citizen's just and tempered treatment of others. We have already seen that at the sexual register, temperance kept Nicocles' desire for pleasure focused within the household, preventing it from reaching out to other women and young boys; similarly, justice kept his desire for gain fixed within the state, preventing him from seizing the lands of his neighboring states. And we heard Nicocles boast to his audience that he behaved unlike other kings who "provide themselves with pleasures from outside their households" (37).

At the economic register the desire for pleasure works in a similar manner, only with far greater consequences. Desiring someone else's possessions is equated with going against one's own interest and neglecting one's affairs at home: "τῶν μὲν οἰκείων ἀμελείας τῶν δ᾽ ἀλλοτρίων ἐπιθυμίας, neglect of their own possessions and of covetousness the possessions of other[s]" (*Peace* 84). Finally, Isocrates unleashes the greatest consequences for a person who, having already violated the norms of temperance, thinks nothing of breaking the rules of justice and, following the impulse to pleasure and gain, reaches out to obtain unjustly what belongs to someone else: "I observe that those who prefer the way of injustice, thinking it the greatest good fortune to seize something that belongs to others, are in like case with animals which are lured by a bait, at the first deriving pleasure from what they seize, but the moment after finding themselves in desperate straits" (*Peace* 34). The desire for pleasure or gain that comes with possessing something not belonging to an individual can lead, if left unrestrained, to a conduct that violates one's identity as citizen. Justice arranges desire on the inside/outside axis so as to differentiate citizens from noncitizens; for only the conduct of a noncitizen could have been compared to the behavior of an animal.

Pursuing pleasure and gain against one's long-range interests does not merely damage the individual citizen but additionally implicates the welfare of the entire polis. Those who "have squandered what they inherited from their fathers on shameful pleasures" have no other choice, Isocrates remarks, than to "seek to repair their own fortunes from the public treasury" (*Panathenaicus* 140). Financial ruin at the personal level puts at risk the welfare of the polis whose well-being is all too often placed in the hands of those who have already led their own households to disaster.[14] When such persons are called upon to administer a public office, it is inevitable that they regard a "charge over public affairs as a chance for private gain" (*Areopagiticus* 25). Hence Isocrates' frequent pleas for moral reform (and in the *Areopagiticus* legal reform) that would teach citizens "not to neglect their own possessions and conspire against the possessions of others, and not to repair their own fortunes out of the public funds" (*Areopagiticus* 24). The desire that has as its target properties or people outside of one's household turns back around and, like a parasite, eats away at the foundation of the entire polity.[15]

Isocrates extends the analogy of the household to the city. His critique of the conduct of the Athenian empire that ended by ruining Athens continues on the axis of care or neglect of one's own household. "For they reached such a degree of neglect of their own possessions and of covetousness of the possessions of other states," he says of the Athenians at the second phase of the Peloponnesian War, "that when the Lacedaemonians had invaded our territory and the fortifications at Decelea had already been built [fourteen miles outside Athens], they manned triremes to send to Sicily and were not ashamed to permit their own country to be cut off and plundered by the enemy while dispatching an expedition against a people who had never in any respect offended against us. Nay, they arrived at such a pitch of folly that at a time when they were not masters of their own suburbs (τῶν προαστείων τῶν οἰκείων) they expected to extend their power over Italy and Sicily and Carthage" (*Peace* 84–85). As with a citizen who follows the desire for pleasure and gain to self-destruction, so with the empire that, reaching out unjustly for what belongs to others, ends up by destroying itself. Hence the desire for undue prosperity, along with its parasitical workings from the inside, provides the point of departure for Isocrates' critique of the Athenian empire: "the wealth which flowed into the city unjustly and which was soon to destroy also that which [could have] justly belonged to it" (*Peace* 83). The wealth Isocrates mentions here must be a reference to the tributes Athens imposed on its allies in a desperate attempt to cover the immense expense of the enormous empire it had built—tributes that, as he notes in the *Panathenaicus*, put an end to the goodwill of the allies (116). This would explain why Isocrates regards the wealth he mentions above as wealth justly belonging to Athens; for, prior to the tributes, the allies would on a voluntary basis give Athens land and cities (cf. *Panathenaicus* 116, *Peace* 140). As with the citizen, then, so with the city: neglect of one's household and pursuit of one's excessive desires for pleasure and gain lead to dire need that can only be met through unjust means, that is, by resorting to a noncitizenly conduct by treating others neither as fellow citizens nor as allies—a conduct, in other words, that inevitably leads to self-destruction.

While the connection between controlling one's desires for immoderate pleasures or excessive gains and running successfully one's affairs or household makes sense—for the citizen and the city alike—it hardly stands to reason that mastery of one's own financial matters or household affairs ought to be regarded as required activity to good oratorical practices. Yet this is a connection Isocrates requires us to make.[16] For, as he claims in the *Antidosis*, his instruction stands to improve people in their handling of both private and public affairs, and the rhetorical education he and his students undertake allows them to "pursue and practice those studies which will enable us to govern wisely both our own households and the commonwealth" (285). In at least one instance he makes the connection himself: "those who are able to manage their affairs from their private incomes are on the side of the commonwealth and of our best councellors" (*Peace* 129).

Why is mastery of one's desires for pleasure and riches a prerequisite for offering sound advice to the city? Why is care of one's household required for speaking as a citizen? Because successful management of one's affairs reduces the possibility that a person's words would originate in selfish motives and that a citizen's advice to the polis would issue out of a personal need. This was the very possibility Aristotle regarded as the duty of lawgivers to eliminate, by seeing to it that only citizens of means would be allowed to run for public offices (*Politics*, 1273b, 1–7). Justice, Isocrates had Nicocles say to his people, is tested "when a man is in want, temperance when he is in power" (44). Depravity breeds a noncitizenly conduct and compels one citizen to look at another not as friend or ally but as source of a potential gain. Words issuing out of depravity and desperation are likely to divide the polis by turning one citizen against the other and by eroding the autonomy and freedom guaranteed to every citizen by the democratic polis.¹⁷ Similarly, advice issuing out of depravity and desperation is likely to erode the city's relation to other cities and ruin alliances founded on mutual trust and respect.

Even though not sufficient for good oratory, then, self-mastery is a necessary condition of good oratory. More important, for Isocrates, it is a condition necessary to deciphering and resisting manipulative oratory. A citizen of means is more likely to draw the line at the point where self-advantage ends and injury to others begins, and not to listen to teachers of oratory who teach "the kind of eloquence which enables people to gain their own advantage contrary to justice" (*Antidosis* 89). Unlike Plato, who proposed dialectic as the sole means of resisting the manipulating and deceptive tactics of Athenian orators,¹⁸ Isocrates offers as antidote the citizen of means as well as, we will see later on, the citizen of intelligence and honor (*Antidosis* 241). Yet, much like Plato, he delivers a scathing critique in the *Antidosis* against the practices of court oratory in his day. Writers of speeches for the courts advertise the fact that "they engage in this training in order that they may defeat the ends of justice in the courts" (229) and create the impression that "cleverness in speech results in plotting against other people's property" (230). Because there is in Athens "a superabundance of men who produce speeches for litigants in the courts" (41), court orators neither "keep their hands off citizens who live soberly" nor "bring before you only those who do evil"; rather, they try to win a competitive edge by "advertiz[ing] their powers in their attacks upon men who are entirely innocent, and so get more money from those who are clearly guilty" (24). Making a livelihood out of challenging contracts between citizens, court orators spend their lives practically living in the courthouses (38) and daily "lay information, hale people into court, and covet the property of others" (99).

The success of court orators lies, according to Isocrates, in their capacity to take advantage of people who have been "brutalized by envy and want" and who, in their desperation, are ready to "wage war, not on depravity, but on prosperity" (*Antidosis* 142). Constrained by need, people become vulnerable to depraved orators and "subservient to the sycophants" (*Peace* 130). In turn, it is this need, along with the excessive desires it fuels, that gives court orators their power: "Wherefore these men would be most happy to see all of our citizens reduced to the condition of helplessness in which they themselves are powerful" (*Peace* 131). This reasoning allows Isocrates to position teachers and practitioners of dicastic oratory outside the boundaries of the citizen as constituted by justice and temperance. Inciting citizen against citizen, orators foster a noncitizenly conduct, so that they may prey on it, ζῆν ἐκ τοῦ συκοφαντεῖν (*Antidosis* 164): "And who more than these sycophants would like to see many of our citizens corrupted and depraved, since they know that when they live among such characters they wield great power" (*Antidosis* 241).

More important, this reasoning permits Isocrates to acknowledge and, at the same time, distance himself from a large segment of oratorical practices that had given the art of rhetoric its ill repute. Critics of the art, Isocrates remarks, "acknowledge that men who take this training are more able, but complain that they are corrupted and demoralized by it, alleging that when they gain the power to do so, they scheme to get other people's property" (*Antidosis* 198). For Gorgias, it sufficed to defend rhetoric as a morally neutral art, open to potential misuse.[19] Isocrates repeats the arguments encountered in the *Gorgias* in defense of arts misused by their practitioners, including the art of boxing. But this line of defense makes up only a brief passage in the *Antidosis* and should not be taken as representative of Isocrates' position; for the case made in the *Antidosis*, in *Against the Sophists*, in *On the Peace*, and in many parts of most of his works is that the version of rhetoric he teaches, in contradistinction to the oratory for the courts, lies within the boundaries of citizenship as constituted by the dialectic of dikaiosyne and sophrosyne. Promoting friendly rather than hostile relations among citizens, strengthening rather than destroying the social fabric of the city, his is a rhetoric of the citizen for the polis.

III

In a letter to Demonicus, Isocrates mentions pleasure and gain as "things by which it is shameful for the soul to be controlled" and asks the monarch to "practice self-control" in both. For, he continues, "it is shameful to rule over one's servants and yet be a slave to one's desires" (*Demonicus* 21). The contradiction between ruling others and being ruled by one's own desires is a favorite theme with Isocrates, especially when he is writing to monarchs. Thus, he reminds Nicocles that he is a king only when he is a slave to no pleasure, and he asks him to rule over his desires more firmly than over his people (*To Nicocles* 29); and he praises Evagoras for having been a master of his pleasures rather than a slave to them (*Evagoras* 45).

From Isocrates' discourse on monarchy we learn that the desire to dominate—like the desire for excessive pleasure or gain—controls, enslaves, and ultimately ruins its author. His advice to monarchs is that they ought to rule (*archein*) but not dominate (*tyrannein*). These terms, he points out in the *Peace*, appear "to have the same meaning, although between them there is the utmost difference." And he offers the following distinction between archein and tyrannein: "it is the duty of those who rule to make their subjects happier through their care for their welfare, whereas it is a habit of those who dominate to provide pleasures for themselves through the labors and hardships of others. But it is the nature of things that those who attempt a despot's course (ἔργοις τυραννικαῖς) must encounter the disasters which befall despotic power and be afflicted by the very things which they inflict upon others" (91). On this distinction Isocrates bases his interpretation of the rise and fall of the Athenian empire. What started out as a legitimate pursuit, he argues, eventually turned into a tyrannical domination that ultimately precipitated in disaster and near slavery: "for in place of holding the citadels of other states, her people saw the day when the enemy were in possession of the Acropolis . . . and in place of farming the lands of other states, for many years they were denied the opportunity of even setting eyes upon their own fields" (*Peace* 92). In the *Areopagiticus* he draws the same conclusion: "because we were anxious about the future and gave attention to our affairs," he says of the Athenians, "we became . . . the foremost of the Hellenes; whereas, when we imagined that our power was invincible, we barely escaped being enslaved" (6). Incidentally, Isocrates also follows this same line of reasoning to interpret the rise and fall of Sparta: "imperialism worked the ruin not only of Athens but of the city of the Lacedaemonians also. . . . Indeed it brought it to pass that a polity which over a period of seven hundred years had never, so far as we know, been disturbed by perils or calamities was shaken and all but destroyed in a short space of time" (*Peace* 95).

Isocrates' interpretation of the Athenian empire requires an account of how a legitimate pursuit for archein can turn into a despotic tyrannein. And we find this account in the extraordinary observation he makes about the difference between the Athenian army and the Athenian navy. According to Isocrates, the army contributed to Athens' ascent to power by creating a sense of safety for the allies that resulted in a hegemony over the other city-states based on their consent; for the allies saw that Athenian "land-power [was] fostered by order and sobriety (*sophrosyne*) and discipline and other like qualities" (*Panathenaicus* 115). The supremacy on land yielded a greater power, and Athens soon gained the supremacy of the sea: "For because of their supremacy on land . . . and of the self-control which was cultivated under it, they readily obtained command of the sea" (*Peace* 102). Once in command of the sea, however, the Athenians, he remarks, "conceived that they were licensed to do whatever they pleased and so were plunged into great confusion (*tarache*)." As a result, "they speedily lost the supremacy both on land and sea" (*Peace* 102). In Isocrates' oration to Philip we see a similar explanation being advanced with the case of Sparta: "because they were persuaded by [Alcibiades] to covet the sovereignty of the sea, they lost even their leadership on land" (*Philip* 61). And the *Areopagiticus* repeats the same conclusion: "the Lacedaemonians . . . made themselves, because they lived temperately and under military discipline, masters of the Peloponnesus; whereas later, when they grew overweening and seized the empire both of the sea and of the land, they fell into the same dangers as ourselves" (7).

To these explanations Isocrates attaches the following moral lesson: "arrogance (*akolasia*) and insolence have been the cause of our misfortunes while sobriety and self-control (*sophrosyne*) have been the source of our blessings" (*Peace* 119). But how can it be that the same power is, at one and the same time, an index of temperance and a sign of arrogance precipitating in confusion? At what point does the power that comes with sophrosyne turn to an akolasia that leads to tarache?

Even though Isocrates does not offer a complete psychological account, he does provide an interesting analysis of the Athenian navy that can help answer these questions. In the *Panathenaicus* he makes this remark about the navy:

a sea-power is not augmented by these [temperance and discipline] but by the crafts which have to do with the building of ships and by men who are able to row them—men who have lost their own possessions and are accustomed to derive their livelihood from the possessions of others. Our fathers did not fail to foresee that with the introduction of these elements into the state the order and discipline of the former polity would be relaxed and that the good will of our allies would soon undergo a change when the Athenians should compel the Hellenes, to whom they had previously given lands and cities, to pay contributions and tribute to Athens in order that she might have the means to pay the kind of men whom I mentioned a moment ago. (116)

The desire to obtain absolute command blinds the Athenians to the point that they turn their welfare over to noncitizens and place their fate willingly in the hands of mercenary outsiders. Elsewhere Isocrates describes mercenary rowers as "vagabonds, deserters, and fugitives who have thronged together here in consequence of other misdemeanours, who, whenever others offer them higher pay, will follow their leadership against us" (*Peace* 44).[20] These are the men, Isocrates continues, for whose sake "we do violence to our own allies and extort money from them in order to provide pay for the common enemies of all mankind" (46).

Power, claims Isocrates, the very thing everyone aspires to attain, is also the most difficult thing to manage: "it turns the heads of those who are enamoured by it" ($\pi\alpha\rho\alpha\phi\rho\rho\nu\epsilon\hat{\iota}\nu$ $\pi o\iota\epsilon\hat{\iota}$ $\tau o\grave{\upsilon}\varsigma$ $\dot{\alpha}\gamma\alpha\pi\hat{\omega}\nu\tau\alpha\varsigma$ $\alpha\dot{\upsilon}\tau\acute{\eta}\nu$) (*Peace* 103). While power can only be obtained through sophrosyne, it turns the person acquiring it from *sophron* to *paraphronon*, from a person in control of desire to a person maddened by it. For the nature of power, Isocrates observes, is similar to the nature of courtesans "who lure their victims to love but destroy those who indulge this passion" (*Peace* 104). The turning point, the shift from legitimate desire to obsession, and from *phronein* to *paraphronein*, is a mental state of confusion (tarache)—the state of mind that comes with the sudden discovery that one is now in the position to gratify any desire at all, as well as the sudden awareness of oneself as the site of a multiplicity of desires (*Areopagiticus* 43). Thus, we are asked to see the Athenians as lovers who, controlled by their obsession to dominate, become blinded to their interests and act in ways that will ensure their self-destruction. Under the state of tarache the Athenians confuse the boundaries that divide citizens from noncitizens and foolishly seek to prop themselves up—and sustain their power—by means of the noncitizen others.

The degree of madness that tarache can lead to is made evident in the following passage on monarchs. When "men obtain unlimited power," Isocrates remarks, "they are compelled to make war upon all their citizens, to hate those from whom they have suffered no wrong whatsoever, to suspect their own friends and daily companions, to entrust the safety of their persons to hirelings whom they have never even seen, to fear no less those who guard their lives than those who plot against them, and to be so suspicious towards all men as not to feel secure even in the company of their nearest kin" (*Peace* 112).

With the Athenians as with the Lacedaemonians, with lovers as with monarchs, the state of confusion that precipitates mad choices and foolish acts is a state of mind brought on solely by oneself. But in the *Philip,* Isocrates links the state of tarache with persuasion. In a brief portrait of Alcibiades he draws for Philip, Isocrates describes the influential Alcibiades as the person who persuaded the Spartans to undertake command of the sea and, as such, the person most responsible for their eventual destruction. As he says to Philip, "the Lacedaemonians, who then appeared to be at the height of their fortune, are [now] reduced to their present state of misfortune,—all on account of Alcibiades. For because they were persuaded by him to covet the sovereignty of the sea, they lost even their leadership on land" (60–61). To serve his own purposes, and return by force back to the land he had been exiled from, Alcibiades looks to the Lacedaemonians for help and finds them obsessed with the desire to rule and, as such, vulnerable to manipulation.[21] It is this vulnerability that gives Alcibiades his power with persuasion. Plunging the Lacedaemonians into a great state of confusion (59), Alcibiades emerges in this passage as the evil persuader par excellence, at once the instigator and beneficiary of tarache.[22]

From Alcibiades' portrait we learn that the desire to dominate creates an opening for persuasion. The drive for pleasure that comes with absolute power does not merely generate an irreversible path toward self-destruction; it additionally sets up the conditions for persuasion that, thriving on confusion and taking advantage of foolishness, expedites the path to self-destruction. In the person of Alcibiades we find only an exaggerated version of what, according to Isocrates, political orators in his day habitually do. Like him, the advice they offer to the polis is motivated by their own selfish purposes, and they stick to these purposes until they succeed in plunging the polis into great confusion. Thus, they advise the polis by fueling its citizens' drive for absolute power, by appealing to their ambition for domination, and by gratifying their desire for excessive pleasure. Orators in the assembly, Isocrates charges, "speak for the gratification of their audience but plunge those who are persuaded by them into many distresses and hardships" (*Panathenaicus* 140). To the Athenians he iterates the same message: "those who say what you desire are able to delude you easily—since what is spoken to win favour clouds your vision of what is best" (*Peace* 10). Like Alcibiades, political orators succeed with attaining their self-interests only to the extent they are capable of destroying the city. Athens' terrible condition began, for Isocrates, "when men of this character took over the supremacy of the rostrum" and when most Athenians lost everything they had "because of the war and of the disorders (tarachai) which these sycophants have caused, while the latter, far from being penniless, have become rich" (*Peace* 121–24).

Isocrates' critique of political orators is based on a view of persuasion with as much power and as many destructive effects as Gorgias had assigned to it. As in Gorgias' *Helen*, the view of persuasion advanced here requires for its triumph a vulnerability on the part of the listeners, the kind of vulnerability that lovers exhibit when under the impulse of a passion they cannot control. In the *Gorgias* the sophist spoke of persuasion as having the power to reduce others to slaves (452e).[23] Isocrates concedes to the destructive effects persuasion can have but takes great care to confine these effects only to those instances when people themselves allow their own desires to control them.

Chapter Three

Human Agency

Constructing political identities in terms of a legal and ethical conduct gave Isocrates a manner of addressing the problem of division at its core, by confronting the gap in the Athenians' self-understanding as individuals and as members of a collectivity.[1] As we saw in the previous chapter, however, the effort to present his version of rhetoric as an art that could forge unity out of division brought Isocrates face-to-face with the perennial problem of classical democracy—the disjuncture that existed, ever since the origin of the democratic polis, between political equality and socio-economic inequality.[2] The disjuncture was so fundamental that it had become part and parcel of the rhetorical tradition Isocrates inherited—a tradition that had originated and continued to evolve against the background of an ongoing tension between political equality and socio-economic inequality. And it is this tradition we may briefly consult as a way of understanding the magnitude of the problem that Isocrates' version of rhetoric had to deal with and attempt to resolve. For if this were to be a rhetoric suited for the fourth-century polis, it would have to offer ways of negotiating the tension that informed one's self-understanding as a human agent, i.e., as a person capable of coming to terms with the disjuncture between reason and emotions, the disparity between individual and collective interests, and the gap between one's political and socio-economic identities.

The previous chapter should have already laid the basis for the present discussion on human agency and should have made amply clear that Isocrates' discourse of citizenship, along with the conduct such discourse prescribes, makes up only one part of the equation. Indeed, while human agency can be perfectly realized through the conduct of a citizen and within the parameters of a behavior regulated by the dialectic of justice and temperance, the version of human agency Isocrates ultimately endorses exceeds the kind of citizenly conduct we have thus far shown him to advocate. With a citizen's conduct, a ruler's leadership, or an orator's practices the discourse of moderation tells only half the story. The other half pertains to the type of agency that obtains when human desire exercises itself in an untempered and immoderate manner. It concerns the third factor of human motivation Isocrates mentioned (the other two being desire for pleasure and desire for gain) and the one we have yet to examine—desire for honor. These two disparate versions, a citizenly conduct based on moderation and a heroic conduct based on excess, give us a more complete portrait of human agency. In addition, they tell the story of Isocrates' complex relation to the tradition of rhetoric; for the effort to orchestrate two disparate versions of human conduct into two constituent parts of human agency involved, as will presently be shown, nothing short of negotiating two drastically different conceptions of rhetoric advanced by two of his predecessors—and the two rhetoricians with the biggest influence on him—Protagoras and Gorgias.

I

Protagoras approached rhetoric as the crux of social life. His great myth of the origins of civilized communities cast logos as the instrument of self-expression as well as the basis of social interaction.[3] For Protagoras, logos allowed each member of the community to express individual needs, interests, and desires. More important, logos additionally provided all members of the community with the opportunity to interact with one another, thereby creating the real possibility that the social order of the community would one day be the direct outcome of the interaction among citizens. But if the rules and regulations that bind the members of the community together are the products of self-expression and communal interaction, then social order becomes not an imposition from the outside but a requirement from within. In this way logos contributes to the production of an order that, far from restraining people, provides the necessary condition for the pursuit of their interests.

Protagoras' theory of logos set into motion the dynamic tension between individuals and community that, he must have felt, was integral to the political life in Athens as he experienced it. In view of the social and economic inequalities that prevailed in Athens during the mid fifth century, Protagoras' notion of the relation of logos to the polis is bound to be regarded as an unrealizable dream.[4] But in view of the equality that dominated political activities in the recently democratized polis, his theory of logos can certainly be taken as the articulation of a wish whose realization was not far away on the political horizon.[5] We should keep in mind that the recent transition from aristocracy to democracy meant, above all else, that Athenian citizens could now participate in the governance of their polis as political equals, regardless of their status in birth or their social and economic attributes. Freed from an order externally imposed by tyrants or aristocrats, citizens could now shape the direction of the polis by participating in its governance, adjudicating its laws, and determining its policies. Freed from a mandatory servitude to rulers' demands, members of the polis could now express their own interests and advocate policies that would serve these interests. Within the climate of optimism that this radical change into participatory democracy undoubtedly created, it is easy to see why Protagoras' words had such a powerful appeal to the Athenians. His construal of logos as a force shaping and ordering political life must have struck a chord with the Athenians by foregrounding a version of themselves they had perhaps already imagined but not yet entertained as possible: a version of themselves as makers of a polis whose shape and direction could now be determined solely by the collective will of its citizenry.

In the context of Athenians' novel attitude toward their polis—as an entity shaped by the interaction among political equals—Protagoras' "man measure" fragment does not pose the kind of insurmountable philosophical difficulties some scholars of classical philosophy have ascertained.[6] For in a society that had just escaped the long grip of an externally imposed order, the statement "man is the measure" expresses not so much a doctrine of absolute relativism as a principle of self-determination.[7] When looked at not as a philosophical treatise but as a rhetorical summons, the "man-measure" proclamation announces the advent of a new epoch in which it will be human beings—not the gods, not the tyrants—who will decide the fate of the polis, who will collectively determine its course of action, and who will take credit or assume responsibility for the outcome. Such a proclamation calls upon citizens to understand themselves as the sole arbiters of individual and communal well-being, and to regard their beliefs, deliberations, and decisions as the only sources of historical agency.

The process of interaction evoked above, of a citizen's self-interests shaping and being shaped by the collective interests of the community, points to a political conception of rhetoric that helps us address the contradictory claims about education attributed to Protagoras. As is well known from Plato's work, Protagoras reportedly claimed for himself the very art he had already given over to the workings of social interaction in the community. Socrates was quick to pick up the contradiction and turn it against his interlocutor: how is it possible, he insists in a lengthy section of *Protagoras*, for someone to claim expertise in the art of political deliberation and at the same time to present that art as a skill that one develops naturally, by simply entering into conversation with other people?

Of the various arguments advanced today in defense of Protagoras, I find Cynthia Farrar's most compelling.[8] The distinction she makes between competence and excellence shows that the contradiction exposed by Socrates is in fact a conflation of two distinct levels of instruction. While everyone in the community is competent to teach the basics of political deliberation to the young and to give advice to the city, only few are talented enough to teach those wishing to become proficient. Hence the case is not as Socrates presented it—that expertise in the art of political deliberation can only lie in a distinct field of technical knowledge or that one's advice to the polis is better than someone else's only to the extent that one can foresee the future better than anyone else. For Protagoras, expertise is not knowledge that renders all other beliefs irrelevant; rather it is an excellence displayed by rendering judgments on the basis of interpreting human experiences consistently with what can be known and in a manner that is convincing to others. In such a view there is room for both competence and excellence, personal opinions and authoritative judgments, competent and superior political advice, plausible and persuasive arguments. Such a view is in line with deliberative practices in the assembly where no single disputant's argument is true or false but where one disputant can defend his interpretations of common experiences more consistently with or more plausibly to what is known. Such a view, finally, leaves room for the teacher of the art of rhetoric to improve the student's ability as regards the persuasiveness and plausibility of arguments. And what better way to do that than to consider both sides of the argument and, in the process, attain proficiency in strengthening the plausibility and persuasiveness of a case that might have initially appeared too weak—in other words, learning how to make the weaker argument stronger.[9]

Protagoras' work, then, looks to the art of rhetoric and to its instruction as offering a viable resolution to the problem of reconciling personal freedom with the requirements of collective life. In providing a forum for the exchange of beliefs among equals, political deliberation fosters an environment in which human excellence is assessed not in terms of birth or wealth but in terms of the capacity to contribute politically to the entire community. Because political deliberation in democratic Athens provides an equal opportunity for every citizen to become a leader, citizens aspire to political excellence by seeking ways to improve on the advice they give to the polis—to make their advice not only subject to their untutored beliefs but also accountable to their own as well as to others' perceptions and judgments of lived experiences. And since some judgments are more plausible and persuasive than others, deliberative practices allow citizens to determine what constitutes political excellence at the same time that they permit political excellence to determine the standards and aspirations of citizens.[10] In this way, the art of deliberation provides the conditions necessary for individual interests to contribute to and be shaped by collective interests, and for the polis to function as the representative and articulator of its citizens' will.

Protagoras' conception of political deliberation, it has already been suggested, urged the Athenians to understand themselves and their relation to their city in ways that were compatible with the possibilities created by the democratization of the polis. It called into existence roles that could be played out, identities that could be inhabited, and notions of citizenship that could be lived out in the world of everyday experience. It promoted, in other words, ways of understanding and experiencing the world that were potentially livable and actualizable. But the link between these forms of living in the world and their potential fulfillment in the polis turned out to be short-lived.

Not long after Protagoras' teachings, the conduct of the Athenian empire toward its allies provided another model of human behavior and a different portrait of political interaction. The extraordinary power of the empire offered a vivid example of what could be attained through sheer strength. Its rapid expansion into a naval superpower that dominated the Mediterranean Sea completely showed to the Athenians that alliance with other city-states stood in the way of Athens' own additional growth, that participation in a common project confined her own potential, and that partnership with other cities restrained her own ambition.[11] Within the context of these new experiences Athenians' notions of community and citizenship, initially promoted by the shift from aristocracy to democracy and subsequently endorsed by Protagoras' notion of political deliberation, were bound to be regarded as obsolete. The virtues of equality and compromise, once seen as requisites to the community's self-determination, were now regarded as constraints imposed upon the few in order to protect the many. Civic laws, once seen as necessary conditions of the freedom to pursue collective interests, were now regarded as arbitrary restrictions and as so many external impositions on the strong in order to safeguard the interests and well-being of the weak.[12] The source of energy for the community, once attributed to cooperation among its members, was now attributed to its few strong members whose power and ambition were unfairly curbed by the interests of the rest. It was within this new climate and this growing awareness of the collective good as no longer representative of individual interests that Gorgias became a celebrated rhetorician.[13]

Gorgias' rhetoric captured the rift inherent in a society that had overthrown political hierarchy but had continued to valorize social and economic hierarchies. His rhetoric appealed to the Athenians' increasing awareness of themselves as individuals rather than as citizens, as social and economic subjects rather than as political agents.[14] Protagoras' dream had been that political virtue would triumph over other personal attributes; that the same equality that structured political life would eventually also structure socio-economic relations; and that all aspects of excellence in the community would be measured by political rather than socio-economic standards. But the rapid expansion of the polis into an empire accountable only to its interests and answerable solely to its will brought about the exact opposite state of affairs. Turning politics into an arena where social aspirations and economic ambitions could materialize efficiently and effortlessly, the conduct of the Athenian empire showed how politics could be used as an instrument to procure precisely those qualities that existing social and economic relations in the polis had always valorized. The imperialistic triumphs of Athens turned Protagoras' vision of politics upside down and showed convincingly that the political was to be construed in terms of the personal and to be measured only by the extent to which it helped obtain individual interests and realize individual desires.

Gorgias' theory of logos as power and of persuasion as seduction reflects the increasing rift in the Athenians' self-understanding qua individuals and qua citizens.[15] Logos, conventionally understood as the expression of a person's freedom and the antithesis of violence and coercion, is now itself regarded as a form of coercion.[16] According to Gorgias, logos provides the basis of an interaction whose net result is not the creation of a social order but the procurement of individual power.[17] An instrument of power, logos works internally by making people willing participants of their own coercion.[18] Specifically, the workings of persuasion follow the operations of seduction: logos offers people a vision of their own good that is so appealing that it compels them to act in the hope of realizing it; by bringing people under the influence of their own beliefs of the good, logos reduces people into slaves of their own desires; the spell cast by logos on people is as powerful as the control exerted by magic over the human soul or as the grip secured by drugs over the human body.[19]

Such a theory of persuasion accounts for the quality of a political life Athenians were becoming accustomed to: the uses of political power for individual gain; the abuses of the deliberating process for personal advantage. That such experiences were possible at all within a democratic community, that people could be persuaded to endorse policies that went against their self-interests, must have brought about the need to reflect on the difference between human beings qua citizens and qua individuals. It is this need for self-reflection that Gorgias' theory of persuasion responded to. The world as he portrays it is a world of individuals compelled by their private desires rather than of citizens motivated by their collective interests. And even though Gorgias does not theorize the difference between the two, his emphasis on individuals as desiring subjects rather than as interested agents makes it possible for readers to infer some key distinctions.

Gorgias problematized the notion of interest by suggesting that there is no essential link tying one's action to one's perceived interest. Even as people entertain what action is in their best self-interest, they are always faced with a sense of doubt: that the act about to be taken might not realize their interests. Connected to the poetic tradition, Gorgias knew too well that such a doubt cannot be erased through good reasoning.[20] The irreconcilable perspectives of tragedy had already demonstrated plainly that the decision to act could not be made on the basis of reason, since both perspectives available to the tragic hero or heroine were by definition equally reasonable and equally convincing.[21] Adapting tragedy's mutually exclusive imperatives for action to the deliberative situation, Gorgias insisted that what propels people to act is not reason but a leap of faith, the taking of a risk, the making of a commitment. To act, people must come under the influence of a belief, a conviction, an impulse.[22] They move in one direction rather than the other because they come to see one alternative as more attractive and one potential version of themselves as more desirable. The gap between the calculations one makes and the action one takes is a gap that only desire can fill.[23]

Gorgias did not give us an explicit theory of political deliberation. But it is easy to see how his theory of persuasion as seduction constituted the polis as an entity that acted not in the face of sound arguments or good reasons attached to a given policy but in view of individual and collective desires. Under him, rhetorical instruction was to develop not along the lines of making arguments consistent with the real or plausible conditions of lived experience, but along the lines of creating arguments that could generate, tap into, and channel human desires. This radical turn in the conception of rhetorical instruction singled out desire as the basis of human deliberation and as the propelling force of collective action. And since appeals to desire do not know the kinds of restraints that appeals to reason must respect, rhetorical instruction assumed an unprecedented amount of freedom.[24] It was the implications of that freedom that Socrates would bring out and condemn in the dialogue *Gorgias*.

To attack Gorgias' conception of human deliberation, Plato singled out the communal actors in the polis whom such a conception reflected, ignoring the communal identities it sought to constitute—hence Plato's well-known portrait of Callicles. A creature of private desires and personal ambition, Callicles is the twin embodiment of desire and power, a person driven by the desire for absolute self-indulgence and looking to power as the means to realize any desire imaginable. He is the orator of the court par excellence, the pedagogue of the assembly amplified to an extreme, one who will use any means to gain a personal advantage and employ any trick to win the argument. As with his critique of Protagoras, here too Plato expresses a similar doubt in people's capacity to construct a social order and to pursue the collective good without a theory of knowledge. But whereas in the former case his critique was directed against people's capacity to form intelligible judgments, his portrait of Callicles sought to annihilate the possibility of erecting anything constructive on the basis of human desire.[25]

It was within this intellectual climate of keen contrast between individuality and collectivity and sharp opposition between desire and reason that Isocrates practiced his art of rhetoric. It was also within a social climate of internal strife and discord, a time when deep conflicts along class lines and political factions divided the polis, that he put forth his rhetorical education. Isocrates joined the general reconstructive efforts of his generation and shared the optimism that the long bygone glory of Periclean Athens could be resurrected—that Athens could regain its lost power and reemerge, if not as the great empire it once was, at least as the formidable leader of a powerful coalition among the Hellenic city-states.[26] It was to the realization of this dream that his instruction of rhetoric was solely devoted.[27]

But such a dream about Athens in the future could not be regarded as possible without some reflection on what might have gone wrong with Athens in the past. The previous chapter describes Isocrates' critique against Athens' handling of the allies and his effort to project notions of uncitizenly conduct onto its foreign policy. To resurrect itself, Athens would have to learn the hard lesson and begin to treat its allies as friends, as well as pattern its own conduct along the lines of conduct it demanded of its citizens. This explains why Isocrates' discourse of human motivation was carried out at both levels—the conduct of the individual and the conduct of the city. We may continue that discussion by examining the third motivational factor Isocrates mentioned: the desire for honor. As will be shown, it is here that Isocrates attempted to close the gap separating individual and collective interests as well as the gap separating Athenian and allied interests.

II

Near the end of *Against the Sophists,* Isocrates declares that "those who desire to follow the true precepts of this discipline may, if they will, be helped more speedily towards honesty of character than towards facility in oratory. And let no one suppose that I claim that just living can be taught; for, in a word, I hold that there does not exist an art of the kind which can implant sobriety (sophrosyne) and justice (dikaiosyne) in depraved natures. Nevertheless, I do think that the study of political discourse can help more than any other thing to stimulate and form such qualities of character" (21). In the *Antidosis* he returns to this passage and offers, this time around, three specific conditions that must be met if his teaching is to lead to an improvement of character. "I do hold," he says, "that people can become better and worthier if they conceive an ambition to speak well, if they become possessed of the desire to be able to persuade their hearers, and, finally, if they set their hearts on seizing their advantage—I do not mean 'advantage' in the sense given to that word by the empty-minded, but advantage in the true meaning of that term" (275).

On closer look at these conditions, it becomes increasingly apparent that the kind of character Isocrates speaks about forging through his instruction is not only the orator fit to practice Isocrates' version of rhetoric but also the political agent, a person capable of negotiating the disjuncture that lies between reason and emotion, the disparity that exists in one's self-interest as individual and as citizen, and the tension that informs one's self-understanding as a political and a socio-economic human being. We can begin our examination of these three conditions by recalling that the final motivation for action Isocrates had offered—in addition to pleasure and gain—and the one left unexamined in the last chapter, is the desire for honor. As will be seen, the key to shaping orators and political agents alike is, for Isocrates, the pursuit of honor and the quest for an honorable reputation.[28]

The desire to earn a good reputation affects one's disposition toward rhetoric. This is already evident in the words Isocrates chose to express the first condition, conceiving an ambition to speak well, πρός τε τὸ λέγειν εὖ φιλοτίμως διατεθεῖεν, which literally means "to dispose oneself toward speaking well as toward seeking after honor." Such a disposition, Isocrates points out, makes it inconceivable that someone "will support causes which are unjust or petty or devoted to private quarrels, and not rather those which are great and honourable, devoted to the welfare of man and our common good" (276). The drive toward a good reputation compels the orator to apply the art of rhetoric to the task of addressing issues that affect everyone's welfare and of proposing solutions to problems that burden the entire polis. And it keeps the orator from approaching the practice of the art as an occasion to benefit the self, the client, or the political party.

The desire for honor positions the orator outside the oratorical practices in the court and the assembly, whose conflictual and divisive nature cannot earn the general esteem of the polis. What an orator can do to prepare for the task of articulating solutions that appeal to everyone or of proposing courses of action that ensure collective benefit, Isocrates does not mention here. But it is clear that he does believe such a preparation to be possible—as the following remark suggests: "he will select from all the actions of men which bear upon his subject those examples which are the most illustrious and the most edifying; and, habituating himself to contemplate and appraise such examples, he will feel their influence not only in the preparation of a given discourse but in all the actions of his life" (277). The turn toward history proposed here, as a way of learning how to guide one's deliberations toward the general good, will be considered in chapter 5.

The second condition to improving character is the orator's desire to persuade audiences. Under the influence of such a desire an orator will be compelled to gain the goodwill of the audience by creating a good name.[29] To become more persuasive, Isocrates claims, the orator cannot but "apply himself above all to establish a most honourable name among his fellow-citizens" (278). Anticipating Aristotle's discussion on the importance of the speaker's ethos to persuasion, especially his remark on moral character as the most effective means of persuasion (*Rhetoric* 1356b), Isocrates links the credibility of the speaker with the speaker's character.[30] But it is the additional link between a speaker's words and past actions that helps Isocrates get around the traditional connection between rhetoric and flattery. He locates the force of persuasion not so much in the words spoken as in the quality of acts performed. As he puts it, "who does not know that words carry greater conviction when spoken by men of good repute than when spoken by men who live under a cloud, and that the argument which is made by a man's life is of more weight than that which is furnished by words" (278).

The conclusion Isocrates draws from this discussion, that "the stronger a man's desire to persuade his hearers, the more zealously will he strive to be honourable and to have the esteem of his fellow-citizens" (278), is a conclusion well prepared for by the discussion in the last chapter about the conduct of a citizen and its importance to good oratory. What is not expected is the sudden invocation of the discourse of erotic love to express the orators' disposition toward persuasion; orators must become, he declares, "possessed of the desire to be able to persuade their hearers" (τοῦ πείθειν δύνασθαι τοὺς ἀκούοντας ἐρασθεῖεν) (275). As seen in the last chapter, Isocrates made use of erotic discourse to acknowledge and expose the manipulative side of persuasion. In this, he showed cognizance of a traditional invocation of eros to express the power of persuasion along the lines of a seductive force that works by capturing the will of hearers and by rendering them indefensible to the will of the aggressor. This explains the traditional portrayal of the effect of persuasion on the mind of the hearer in terms parallel to the effect of eros on the soul of the beloved: at once the creation of tarache and the persuasive use of tarache to gain unfair advantage.

Why resort to a well-encoded metaphorics in order to express something entirely different? Why link *peitho* (persuasion) and eros together in order to capture the speaker's desire to establish a good reputation in the polis? I am inclined to understand this as one more instance in which Isocrates follows Plato's lead and uses Plato's insight in order to break away from rhetoric's traditional reputation, even as he appropriates the philosopher's insight to rhetorical ends. In the *Phaedrus* Plato took such a lead with the discourse of erotic love by shifting the site of madness that comes with being in love from the beloved to the lover. For Plato this was a necessary move; he had to speak of the lover as someone madly inspired by love if he were ultimately to establish love as a deity.[31] And this inspiration, which Plato describes as a state of madness, is to be distinguished from the traditional madness of the beloved—a state that leaves the beloved vulnerable to the lover's manipulative control.[32] Under the condition of being in love, Plato says, the lover's soul "esteems [the beloved] above all others, forgets for him mother and brothers and all friends, neglects property and cares not for its loss, and despising all the customs and proprieties in which it formerly took pride, it is ready to be a slave" (252a). The beloved, in turn, grants conversation and intimacy to the lover, since the former "receives all service from his lover, as if he were a god, and since the lover is not feigning, but is really in love" (255a).

The evidence is simply not there to assert that Isocrates is in fact proposing that the pursuit of good reputation can only come with treating the polity as the honorable lover, possessed by love, would treat the beloved. Nevertheless, there are several indications to support the suggestion that Isocrates might be attempting to link persuasion with eros in a new way—so that persuasion is no longer exclusively thought of as a technique of capturing and enslaving hearers for the sake of obtaining one's own advantage, but rather as a way of realizing noble causes one is dedicated to and is prepared to serve wholeheartedly, especially causes promoting the common good. For one, he refers to peitho as a goddess (*Antidosis* 249) and to persuasion as a gift from the gods (*Antidosis* 247). For another, he speaks of citizenship as a service to the community (*Antidosis* 161, 165, 305; *Areopagiticus* 25, 27) and of good orators as benefactors to the polis (*Antidosis* 144, 231). Finally, the state of being possessed by the desire to persuade makes most sense in the context of the third condition, according to which the drive for good reputation positions someone directly against one's immediate interests. The self-renunciation demanded by the pursuit of good reputation, not unlike that which is demanded of the lover, can only be met through excessive desire. And how better to capture this excess than by using the discourse of erotic love, whose conventional codification of desire as madness makes self-denial plausible?[33]

Isocrates describes his notion of true advantage—the third condition to establishing an honorable character—in a manner echoing Socrates: "those are better off now and will receive the advantage in the future at the hands of the gods who are the most righteous and the most faithful in their devotions, and . . . those receive the better portion at the hands of men who are the most conscientious in their dealings with their associates, whether in their homes or in public life, and are themselves esteemed as the noblest among their fellows" (*Antidosis* 282). This is not the only occasion when Isocrates makes overtures to a Socratic way of life. He alludes to it in reference to his own lifestyle (*Antidosis* 149) and to the lifestyles of those he respects (*Antidosis* 228). And in at least one passage he echoes Socrates' teaching, claiming that the attainment of virtue results in the procurement of worldly goods: "They fail to see that nothing in the world can contribute so powerfully to material gain, to good repute, to right action, in a word, to happiness, as virtue and the qualities of virtue. For it is by the good qualities which we have in our souls that we acquire also the other advantages of which we stand in need" (*Peace* 32).

The contradiction that emerges between the passages above, which urge servitude to the point of self-denial, and the passages noted in the last chapter, which urged mastery over one's affairs and possessions, becomes resolved when we take a closer look at Isocrates' notion of reputation. For Isocrates, we must recall, reputation (*doxa*) is conferred by either one of two conducts, temperance (sophrosyne) or honor (*time*).

As seen in the previous chapter, temperance is associated with self-control, restraint, and moderation. The reputation that comes with temperance, as in the case of the power Athenians earned through the discipline of their army or in the case of citizens able to manage their affairs with care and self-restraint, is slow and gradual.[34] In private affairs as in the affairs of the city, Isocrates remarks, people must "emulate the judgment of such men . . . who prefer a moderate competence with justice to great wealth unjustly gained." For it was these men, he goes on, who eventually "handed on the city to their descendants in a most prosperous condition and left behind them an imperishable memorial of their virtue" (*Peace* 93–94).

Isocrates' discourse on a reputation that comes with temperance follows the logic of a sound investment.[35] Always linked to a citizenly conduct (moderation for oneself and consideration for others), always respecting boundaries of friendship or alliance, the drive for reputation banks on the payoffs that tempered conduct at present will be certain to yield in the future. These payoffs include pleasure, gain, and power, i.e., the very things that tempered conduct militates against. But like a sound investment, the pleasure, gain, and power that are conferred through reputation are far more abundant and durable. Isocrates' advice to Demonicus with regard to pleasure reads as follows: "Pursue the enjoyments which are of good repute (τὰς ἡδονὰς τὰς μετὰ δόξης); for pleasure attended by honour is the best thing in the world, but pleasure without honour is the worst" (17). Isocrates' advice to the Athenians with regard to power also supports his discourse: we will become truly powerful, he remarks near the end of the *Peace*, only if we are willing "to treat our allies just as we would our friends and not to grant them independence in words, while in fact giving them over to our generals to do with as they please, and not to exercise our leadership as masters but as helpers . . . [but] to consider that nothing is more important . . . than to have a good name among the Hellenes. For upon those who are so regarded they willingly confer both sovereign power and leadership" (τὰς δυναστείας καὶ τὰς ἡγεμονίας) (134–35). Reputation earned through temperance is, for Isocrates, the key to real power, the only way of aligning together the ordinarily antithetical forces of dynastic rule and hegemonic leadership. The mere thought about such a reputation turns Isocrates into a visionary. In his words, "what city or what men will not be eager to share our friendship and our alliance when they see that the Athenians are at once the most just and the most powerful of peoples and are at the same time both willing and able to save the other states, while needing no help for themselves? What a turn for the better should you expect the affairs of our city to take when we enjoy such good will from the rest of the Hellenes? What wealth will flow into Athens when through her all Hellas is made secure?" (*Peace* 139–40).

The logic of investment, on which Isocrates' discourse on reputation through temperance is based, makes use of such binaries as apparent and real advantage, false and true self-interest; and it organizes these binaries on an axis of temporality—the present: effortless, quick, ephemeral; as opposed to the future: laborious, slow, durable. It is on these binaries and this temporal axis that Michel Foucault's analysis of the discourse on moderation has focused to make his case about a radical shift in Classical Greece.[36] Based on a number of diverse discourses, from Plato's discourse on love to various discourses on health, medicine, and homosexuality, Foucault's conclusion—that what we have here is a new discursive formation, an anticipation of the discourse of Christianity that came to be known as the discourse of self-renunciation—is rather convincing. It certainly does have explanatory power as regards Isocrates' discourse on reputation based on temperance.

Yet this is only half of the story, for even as it promotes the curbing of excessive desires, the discourse on reputation is—in Isocrates' case—frequently driven by excess. All three conditions for improving one's character, in fact, are anchored on that person's excessive desire for self-improvement. Let us take another look at the entire passage: "But I do hold that people can become better and worthier if they conceive an ambition to speak well (πρός τε τὸ λέγειν εὖ φιλοτίμως διατεθεῖεν), if they become possessed of the desire to be able to persuade their hearers (τοῦ πείθειν δύνασθαι τοὺς ἀκούοντας ἐρασθεῖεν), and, finally, if they set their hearts on seizing their advantage (πρὸς τούτοις τῆς πλεονεξίας ἐπιθυμήσαιεν)" (Antidosis 275). The verbs used in the passage—"to conceive," "to become possessed," "to set one's heart on"—are in the original variants of the verb "to desire." More than that, they are verbs that rhyme. Thus, the passage artistically performs the excess it conveys through repetition.

This brings us to the other half of the story—Isocrates' notion on reputation as the outcome of one's pursuit of glorious deeds. Such a pursuit is made possible by means of an innate boldness, a natural proclivity toward danger, and an exceptional drive for distinction. Bold, dangerous, and ambitious undertakings gave Athens the reputation it once enjoyed: "I think that honour is due to our ancestors no less for their wars than for their other benefactions; for not slight, nor few, nor obscure, but many and dread and great, were the struggles they sustained, some for their own territories, some for the freedom of the rest of the world" (Panegyricus 51–52). Reputation that accrues from bold undertakings is, at least according to one passage, more highly esteemed than reputation earned through selfless services rendered to others. As he argues in the Antidosis, "far greater honour is due to [Athens] for the perils she has faced in war than for her other benefactions" (58).

The daring and boldness required for private distinction and personal reputation are natural traits, signs of a particular physis. Thus Zeus "granted the gift of nature" to Helen "knowing that all distinction and renown accrue, not from a life of ease, but from wars and perilous combats" (Helen 17). And Isocrates' appeal to Philip to assume the leadership of Hellas in a war against Asia is made on the grounds of Philip's daring nature: "men of high purposes and exceptional gifts ought not to undertake enterprises which any of the common run might carry out with success, but rather those which no one would attempt save men with endowments and power such as you possess" (Philip 41). Finally, the glory attained by Theseus, who united the scattered residents of Attica into the Athenian city-state, and the fame won by Agamemnon, who united the warring Greeks in a common expedition against Troy, are entirely due to the daring nature and uncompromising ambition of their person (*Helen* 31; *Panathenaicus* 76).

Far from calling for self-control and self-restraint, the discourse on a reputation that comes with undertaking noble deeds thrives on excessive desire and immoderate ambition. In fact, the possibility of attaining such a reputation becomes a mechanism for unleashing immodest desires and fueling excessive ambition. Thus, Isocrates' appeal to the Athenians to undertake a united expedition against Asia in the *Panegyricus* comes with a reminder of the reputation that awaits them, should they partake in this glorious expedition: "And how great must we think will be the name and the fame and the glory which they will enjoy during their lives, or, if they die in battle, will leave behind them—they who will have won the meed of honour in such an enterprise" (186). Far from invoking the ancestors' deeds as an example for emulation, the discourse on reputation looks to ancestors' celebrated conduct as a mark to be surpassed.[37] "Consider," Isocrates tells Philip, "how worthy a thing it is to undertake, above all, deeds of such a character that if you succeed you will cause your own reputation to rival that of the foremost men of history" (*Philip* 68).

III

The two distinct discourses on reputation confirm Isocrates' sensitivity to the dual character of human agency—the individual need for personal glory and fame as well as the public need for civic distinction and recognition. Alongside self-mastery and moderation, there is also excessive desire and immodest ambition. Concurrent with Isocrates' effort to persuade the Athenian youth to embrace a life of temperance and virtue (*Antidosis* 288), there is his endeavor "to inspire them to a life of valour and of dangers endured for their country" (*Antidosis* 60). Next to his admonitions to the Athenians in the *Peace* to assume a life of temperance, there appear in the *Panegyricus* his calls for war, danger, and glory. Against his appeal to Nicocles to temper his rule and exercise control over pleasure, there is his appeal to Philip to expand his rule and to indulge in the most extreme form of pleasure, that "of surpassing joys and of imperishable honours" (*Philip* 71). His effort to reconcile the historical contradiction he inherited—the Athenians' split self-understanding as political and socioeconomic agents—cannot be located in an attempt to suffocate individual impulses by the collective or to curb individual desires by means of a higher or a truer collective reasoning. Nor can it be located in an attempt to valorize personal desires and individual pursuits of glory at the expense of or independently from the public good. Rather it must be sought in the effort he exerted to construct human agency as doubly shaped by the dialectics of desire and reason, reckless ambition and calculated risk, madness and prudence. Such a construction of human agency is sustained, as will be seen in chapter 5, by a version of rhetoric well suited to deliberate the good and the possible for the polis, a rhetoric equally guided by reason and desire.

Gunther Heilbrunn saw the makings of that rhetoric and, in a brilliant article, divided Isocrates' works into prowar and propeace orations, encomia and admonitions, artistic innovations and inartistic collages of familiar maxims.[38] In his words, there "seems to be present continuously in Isocrates a tension between the summons to war and the desire for power, and the need for self-restraint and sobriety" (173). According to Heilbrunn, the first group of works is animated by the rhetoric of seduction, a rhetoric that plays on the collective desires of the Athenians, seduces them with mythical images of glory and power, intoxicates them with visions of immortality, and leads them to war against the Persians. By contrast, the second group is animated by the rhetoric of sobriety and moderation, a rhetoric that curtails the desire for power, curbs the ambition for personal glory, and urges pacification and civic reform.

The two distinct rhetorics Heilbrunn identifies confirm the argument this study has been making all along: that Isocrates' rhetoric is informed by two distinct versions of rhetoric, Protagoras' and Gorgias'. Heilbrunn's classification is justifiable, therefore, only insofar as it discerns the two veins of the rhetorical tradition that traverse Isocrates' works: the rhetoric of prudence and civic reform; and the rhetoric of power and seduction. It is too rigid, however, as regards the possibility that Isocrates may have appropriated the rhetorical tradition to his own ends, and may have indeed combined the two traditions he had inherited into a single, indissolubly unique rhetoric. Only a combination of Protagoras' and Gorgias' rhetorics would have been appropriate to respond to the complexities of human agency he sought to resolve—the capacity to come to terms with the oppositional demands of civic renown and personal glory, to negotiate the contradictory impulses of reason and desire, and to orchestrate the antithetical pulls of political and socio-economic identities. Isocrates' project was an ongoing effort to channel the awesome power of persuasion that Gorgias had unleashed in the direction of the polis, and thereby strengthen Protagoras' effort to make rhetoric the true art of political deliberation.

Chapter Four

Eloquence and Reflection
Antidosis

In the first chapter I mentioned in passing that Isocrates' hymn to logos may also be regarded as a possible critique against the deliberating practices of Athenian orators in his day. And in the second chapter we saw that critical strand develop further as Isocrates relegated political oratory outside the boundaries of justice and moderation and constructed political orators as speaking from outside the ethical bounds of citizenship. In the meantime, in chapter 3 we witnessed Isocrates expending the efforts to appeal to Athenians as political agents and to construct human agency politically, i.e., in a manner that would negotiate the tension between individual and collective interests, all of which has paved the way for us to examine presently what alternative to political oratory Isocrates offers. Such an examination could not be regarded as complete without an accompanying inquiry into Isocrates' own practice—an inquiry which will be undertaken in chapter 5 as we take a close look at *Panegyricus,* his best-known political oration. Before turning to an actual speech, however, it may be fruitful to examine Isocrates' version of political oratory broadly, in relation to the oratorical practices in his day.

Any such examination is bound to fall within the spacious categories of Werner Jaeger, who attributed Isocrates' uniqueness as rhetorician to the distinct ethico-political orientation he gave to oratorical practices as he directed the art of rhetoric toward "the world of politics and ethics."[1] According to Jaeger, Isocrates worked out "a more profound conception of the purpose of rhetorical education than had ever existed before," a working out which "shifted the emphasis from style and form to the content of the 'advice' that the orator imparts. . . . And the content, the subject of rhetoric, is the world of politics and ethics" (90). What is astonishing about Jaeger is that he did not hesitate to attribute to Isocrates a radical break from the history of rhetoric, even though he wrote during the era of formalism and his narrative about *paideia* was largely informed by Hegel's theory of history. Nevertheless, the break in the rhetorical tradition he assigned to Isocrates was not carried across all the registers of his inquiry. His chapter on "The Prince's Education," with its emphasis on rhetorical education as a training for leaders, situated Isocrates' rhetoric within the parameters of self-representation—a position already opened up and made available for rhetorical education by the Sophists. In this way Jaeger's point about the new space opened up by Isocrates, a space that situated orators in the position of giving advice, loses its transformative edge as soon as we begin to distinguish Isocrates from his predecessors along the lines of the content of the advice offered while presuming all along that the gesture of giving advice bears, in both cases, an identical relation to political practices in Athens.

But the space that Isocrates opened up for rhetoric can no longer be recognized from within the paradigm of self-representation; indeed, it makes a radical departure from it. For the link he attempted to establish between his version of rhetoric and the welfare of the polis sought to alter not only the character of the art he had inherited and its traditional role within Athenian politics but also, as we will see, the very character of political life in Athens. Indeed, we stand to miss the entire thrust of Isocrates' relation to the tradition of rhetoric unless we see his version of rhetoric as being erected on a new conception of the political.

I

Most surprising is the ease with which Isocrates severed rhetoric from the two spheres of activity, the court and the assembly, in which the art had traditionally flourished. It was these two public domains that had given rhetoric its raison d'être ever since the art had been imported to Athens around the mid fifth century.[2] From the advent of the Sophists to the time of Plato, instruction in rhetoric had steadily evolved around the requirements of private litigation and political deliberation, and Athenians had continued to regard the art as a means of defending their interests in an increasingly complex world. The rapid changes in the legal and legislative domains effected by the equally rapid process of democratization had created a need no other art could address or respond to.

This is no place to recount the long process of democratization in Athens and its effects on legal and legislative domains.[3] Yet it is impractical to talk about innovation without giving some broad sense of the historical background against which the "new" can be read as innovative. It might be worthwhile, therefore, to pause here and take a brief look at the rhetorical practices Isocrates inherited and their relation to the democratic institutions in Athens. For rhetoric had evolved alongside a fluctuating democracy whose ongoing restructuring of the courts and the assembly continued to make the process of decision-making in both arenas increasingly more conducive to the art of speaking well, or *eu legein.* By the mid fifth century the authority to make legal decisions on constitutional, public, and private affairs had been completely handed over to juries who were selected by lot.[4] Each year some six thousand jurors were chosen and distributed to various courts, usually five hundred jurors per court, though some important cases were tried by as many as two thousand jurors. And since the verdict of juries was final, the legal authority commanded by ordinary citizens was supreme. As Aristotle put it in the *Athenian Constitution,* the law-court adjudicates everything, both public and private, hence, when the people controls the vote, it controls the constitution (9.1).

Also by the mid fifth century the council, whose traditional function was to coordinate the administrative work of the magistrates, had lost its governing power. Since the constitutional reforms of Kleisthenes the council had been required to defer to the assembly decisions involving most political issues, and soon after that the council's function had been reduced to the mere setting of the agenda for the assembly.[5] The administration of the state was entrusted almost entirely to magistrates chosen by lot, the most crucial exception being the election of the ten generals who commanded the army and the fleet and who exercised a general control over the implementation of citizens' decisions regarding foreign policy. All political decisions, including the decision to wage war, were consigned to a majority vote in the assembly, which was open to any Athenian citizen willing to attend and, when important decisions were to be made, regularly drew an attendance of over five thousand people.

Within this democratic system speech became the heart of the city's judicial and political life. Carrying within itself the impulse of democracy, speech no longer drew its power from the social or religious authority of the speaker: words did not rule because the king had spoken them; nor did words establish the truth because the high priest had uttered them. Removed from the private sphere of the king's court and the secret practices of religious cults, speech was relegated to the procedures of an open society and to the deliberations of a public.[6] Legal and legislative issues were submitted to open debate and public argument, and they had to be resolved at the conclusion of a contest in words. The public, to which speech was addressed, listened to arguments and debates and made a conclusive ruling. No aspect of the judicial and political life of Athens remained unaffected by its contact with public speaking; no aspect of the democratic polis remained impervious to the art of oratory.

In the meantime, the sociopolitical instability of Athens following the death of Pericles and the economic devastation of the city-state at the aftermath of the Peloponnesian Wars contributed to a volatile climate of conditions that created an ever higher incentive for citizens to seek some training in the art of eu legein. Eloquence in speaking publicly became increasingly linked to social success, and rhetorical education came to be regarded as an instrument of upward mobility, a ticket to swift political fame, a means to instant economic gain.[7] With Pericles' death came the end of an era, a long period of aristocratic control over political leadership. Even during Pericles' time the tradition of drawing leaders from upper-class families was upheld. It sufficed for aristocratic youth to educate themselves in the technical skills of military and naval warfare that their prospective offices would require. With the death of Pericles, Aristotle remarks in the *Athenian Constitution*, Athenian leadership underwent an irreversible change, as a new class of leaders emerged (28.1). These were leaders, M. I. Finley explains, who were wealthy, perhaps as wealthy as their predecessors, but who had made their wealth with no ties to an aristocratic lineage. They formed a new class not because they came from the ranks of the poor but because they brought a democratic outlook to Athenian politics that broke the aristocratic monopoly of leadership. They rose to power, Finley remarks, by "accepting democratic institutions and offering themselves as leaders, an offer that the *demos* did not reject or resist" (*Politics* 31).

Whether or not we accept Finley's effort to explain this new class of leaders along noneconomic class lines, it is hard to imagine how a monopoly of leadership could have been broken by a mere new "offer." It is more likely that the new leaders did not merely offer themselves as such but had to argue their case vehemently before the demos. This is, after all, the portrait depicted by Aristotle, who points to Cleon as "the first person to use bawling and abuse on the platform, and to gird up his cloak before making a public speech, all other persons speaking in orderly fashion," and who describes the line of leaders following Cleon as "an unbroken line by the men most willing to play a bold part and to gratify the many with an eye to immediate popularity" (28.3–4). The quality of leadership notwithstanding, the democratic structure of the assembly attributed eloquence a role all too evident. In the political era following Pericles' reign, speech competed against aristocratic blood for political authority. And in this contest, as Vernant points out, it was inevitable that speech would win: "The system of the polis implied, first of all, the extraordinary pre-eminence of speech over all other instruments of power. Speech became the political tool par excellence, the key to all authority in the state, the means of commanding and dominating others" (*Origins* 49).

In the judicial system economy played a more profound role and had an impact that was much easier to document.[8] For the task of prosecution was now consigned to volunteers, and a successful prosecution was rewarded with significant amounts of money. One type of case (*apographe*) involved the prosecution of anyone who retained in his possession property belonging to the state. If the prosecutor, who could have been any citizen, won the case, he was awarded three-quarters of the value of the property.[9] A successful litigant would receive one-third of the property of the offender in another type of case (*graphe*) and in other cases (*phasis*) one-half the amount that the defendant was obliged to pay.[10] Needless to say, this encouraged litigation, especially against the rich. Aristophanes depicts the rise of a whole group of people (*sycophants*) who made their living by prosecuting others.

Whether or not they sought the study of rhetoric in order to learn how to defend themselves against actual and potential litigants or demagogues, Athenians looked to the art of eu legein as a means of self-representation and to its instruction as training in safeguarding their interests. By the time of Isocrates, rhetorical education had linked itself securely with the two spheres of activity in which self-representation mattered the most. It was rhetoric's long and successful connection to effective self-representation that had made the art of eu legein so popular among the Athenians. Parallelly, the thin line that separates the uses of the art for self-representation from the abuses of the art for self-advancement, a line that teachers and practitioners of rhetoric had crossed over many times, had given the art its notoriety. Plato's persistent and powerful attacks on rhetoric are reliable indicators that some Athenians pushed toward self-advancement at all costs. Neither justice nor competence stood in the way of opportunists who looked to rhetoric as a means to economic gain or a ticket to political power.

II

A product of his times, Isocrates seems to have started out his career as a logographer, a writer of speeches for the courts. He earned his living by selling his services to Athenian citizens who, having to represent themselves as litigants or defendants and wanting to ensure the best self-representation possible, chose to hire specialists in court oratory and to voice their pleas in court by reading speeches prepared for them in advance.[11] Like so many other rhetoricians with nonaristocratic origins, Isocrates took his craft to a sphere of public activity where the demand for oratory was at its heaviest. And his earliest efforts at becoming a rhetorician coincided with the structure of the profession at the time. The professional identity he sought was an identity already in place and available to anyone who could adapt the art of speaking eloquently to the legal demands of self-representation. In his professional pursuits as in his practices of rhetoric, he followed the direction that the professionalization of the art had already taken: the blending together of eloquence with legal knowledge into a craft responsive to the ongoing demands of self-representation created by the continuing process of democratization of Athenian courts as well as by the constant changes in laws.

The dates of Isocrates' six extant court speeches (from about 402 to 392) and the date he opened his school (around 390, about four years before Plato founded the Academy) suggest that his ten-year-old profession as speech writer had been lucrative enough to enable him to change professions from logographer to teacher of rhetoric. Soon after he opened his school, he seems to have grown wealthy from fees and gifts he received from his students.[12] Having reached financial independence, Isocrates was never again to write speeches for the courts, and, growing increasingly more embarrassed about his early profession, he eventually denied ever having been a logographer.[13]

His new profession enabled him to pursue rhetorical practices outside the domain of the art's established uses and beyond its mainstream applications in the court and the assembly. Under his instruction the art of rhetoric was to take a new direction and to develop by its association with general concerns of political life. Rhetoric was to abandon its traditional links with legal and legislative practices and cultivate new ties with the general welfare of citizens and the overall future direction of the polis. Eloquence was to come in contact with issues of importance to all citizens, and to flourish through discourses that demonstrated dexterity with language by addressing subjects "of superior moral worth" (*Helen* 12) and entertaining "questions of public welfare" (*Antidosis* 80). And persuasion was to disengage itself from private disputes in the court or the narrow demands of policy making in the assembly and instead direct citizens' awareness to issues dealing "with affairs of state" (*Antidosis* 46) and requiring everyone's attention.

The new mission Isocrates gave rhetoric placed the art outside the dynamics of self-representation and beyond the charges of immoral opportunism. His uniqueness as a rhetorician lies in his approach to the art of rhetoric as a practice inextricably tied to the welfare of the polis. No aspect of rhetoric he cultivated remained outside the purview of a desire on his part to link rhetoric with the polis and make rhetorical practices responsive to the demands of political life in Athens. As he exclaimed in the *Antidosis*, it is the affairs of the polis (τὰ κοινὰ τῆς πόλεως) that should be the object of our toil, our study, and our every act (285).

This new turn was based on his conception of rhetoric as the art of discerning and expressing the best courses of action available to the polis, provided that "best" is understood as those pertaining both to the moral and the expedient. Indeed, he called for a political oratory that would integrate choices about values with choices about action and that would advocate courses of action based on the best moral and political alternatives. Political oratory, in other words, rested for Isocrates on the capacity to undertake an ethico-political inquiry, a deliberation by means of which ethical choices illuminated decisions about action and choices regarding political action illuminated decisions about ethical commitments. Erected on deliberation about ethical and expeditious choices, rhetoric for Isocrates was an indistinguishably ethical and political art—the art of making sound choices about the politically possible and the ethically available.

A conception of rhetoric based on a deliberation of the good and the possible commits us to articulating Isocrates' view of rhetorical education as instruction in making sound ethical and political judgments. Indeed, this is the objective that will be defended in the final chapter as the most central goal of Isocrates' rhetorical education. His was, as we will see, an instruction in how to discern the good and the possible for the polis. Yet, before Isocrates could claim that he could impart to others the ability to deliberate intelligently or the power to discern insightfully, he had to augment the art of eloquence with intelligence and thought. Thucydides had once described the ideal of democracy as an interactive process between intelligent argument and insightful judgment: "the best councellors are the intelligent, and the best at listening to and judging arguments are the many" (6.39.1). And Isocrates, who claimed to teach rhetoric for both public and private use—i.e., for those who sought to become politicians as well as for those who merely wanted to educate themselves and presumably develop their capacity to assess the arguments made by politicians—had to dissociate rhetoric from its reputation as mere eloquence and link it instead to an eloquence supported by intelligence and good judgment. The beginnings of such an effort have already been traced to the hymn to logos, in which Isocrates claims that the power of logos to guide is best used by the wise: "in all our actions as well as in all our thoughts speech is our guide, and is most employed by those who have the most wisdom" (9).

Isocrates cast rhetoric as an art that combined eloquence with wisdom and presented his instruction as training in eu legein and phronein.[14] His explicit goal was to cultivate his students' ability to speak eloquently and think intelligently, and his educational program placed on the cultivation of intelligence no less emphasis than on the cultivation of eloquence. Eloquence and wisdom appear frequently in the *Antidosis* as two parts of the same phrase (*legein kai phronein*) as well as two qualities of the same power; those who study under him diligently and zealously will be awarded, he proclaims in the *Antidosis,* by the power of eloquence and wisdom (277). The link of legein to phronein was essential to the new political mission of rhetoric. For if rhetoric were to deal with subjects of concern to all citizens and to address issues of consequence for the entire polis, the tradition of the art (eloquence as *eu legein*) would have to be supplemented by the ability to make sound judgments. In the *Panathenaicus* Isocrates spoke retrospectively about his own practice, reminding his audience that he had written not on "things about which the other orators prate, but the affairs of Hellas and of kings and of states" (11). The topics to which the practice of eloquent speaking attaches itself alter its character; those who speak "upon questions of public welfare," he points out in *Antidosis* (80–81), need to have not only dexterity with words but also "superior qualities of mind" (*psyche phronimotere*). If rhetoric were to dissociate itself from petty, trivial, and inconsequential topics, if it were to take as its subject matter issues of national importance and public consequence, then a link between eloquence and wisdom seemed inevitable. For eloquence alone, no matter how masterful, would not be sufficient to meet the requirements of an art that purported to address meaningfully questions of lasting importance.

The link between eloquence and wisdom forged a discursive practice so unique that no proper name could be attached to it—hence Isocrates' difficulty in putting a label on his teaching. The term *rhetoric* would have connected him too closely to teachers of oratory for whom, like Plato, rhetoric meant the art of eloquence applied to the specific oratorical demands in the courts and the assembly. Thus he opted for the term *philosophy*. As he said to a friend of his, "you are eager for education and I profess to educate; you are ripe for philosophy and I direct students of philosophy" (*To Demonicus* 3). Like *rhetoric*, the term *philosophy* carried its own associations and baggage. From Callicles but also from Isocrates himself we hear repeatedly that while the study of philosophy is something honorable when pursued by youths, it becomes something shameful when sought after by older people. Isocrates' choice of *philosophy* suggests that the term at that time was neither as rigid in connotation nor as fixed in meaning as the term *rhetoric*.[15]

Still, it is important to point out that Isocrates used *philosophy* in its most basic sense, as reflection, and understood phronein as reflection concerning not ideas per se but practical affairs. By bringing phronein in contact with legein, he made the affairs of the polis the object of reflection and gave wisdom a practical orientation. It is also important to point out that, in its contact with reflection, eloquence also underwent a substantive change, for it was subjected to a new concept of time. With Isocrates, impromptu speaking ceased to be a mark of an accomplished orator. The familiar sophistic practice of exhibiting one's art by boasting readiness to speak on any subject and by inviting auditors to name any topic on which they wanted to hear a speech underwent a serious critique. So did the art's

link to improvisation and the practice of orators to study the art by building a repertoire of commonplace topics that they could then use as guides
to improvisation.[16]

This was, then, one of Isocrates' most important contributions to the
history of rhetoric: he gave to the art the gift of time. Away from the courtroom and outside the general assembly, rhetoric was no longer constrained by a sense of urgency and, in the absence of that constraint, did
not have to sacrifice its artistic integrity to the contingent demands of a
client's interests. Released from the pressures imposed by the waterclock
in the courtroom and the protocols of debating in the assembly, delivered
from the burden of an advocacy tied exclusively to the recommendation
of a policy or a verdict, eloquence pursued outside the court and far from
the assembly could, Isocrates felt, be shaped by an art whose exigency
would be determined by the general condition of the polis rather than by
the contingent demands of a private interest or a personal issue. More
closely tied now to the cultural and the thematic,[17] eloquence could afford
the time it needed to become an art. With time on its side, eloquence
would have a chance to develop its intrinsic qualities even as it continued
to cater to an external situation, and to become a self-sufficient art even as
it continued to be shaped by a purpose outside its form. This is what
Isocrates was pointing to through his praising remarks of an art "akin to
works composed in rhythm and set to music" and of an effort to "set forth
facts in a style more imaginative and more ornate" or "employ thoughts
which are more lofty and more original" or "use throughout figures of
speech in greater number and of more striking character" (*Antidosis* 47).
For such artistic efforts, Isocrates goes on, can only come from those who
"have drawn from their pursuit of wisdom the eloquence which I have
described" (48). Putting eloquence in the service of capturing "the right
sentiments" and "set[ting] them forth in finished phrase" is, Isocrates concludes, "the peculiar gift of the wise" (*Panegyricus* 9). And the practitioners of this kind of art do not merely produce a greater pleasure in their
listeners but are also esteemed by their auditors to be "wiser and better
and of more use to the world" (*Antidosis* 48).

The link between legein and phronein did not merely transform the
aesthetic character of rhetoric. For the aesthetic drew its purpose solely
from the political, even as it refigured politics in broader terms, as deliberation about "common concern" or "public issues,"[18] rather than politics
construed in the narrow sense by established practices in the assembly, as
deliberation about policy. Political oratory—now reconceived as political
discourse[19]—was thought to be eloquent only to the extent that it could
convey to citizens artistically the import of the political issue it addressed.
And it was thought to be wise solely by the extent to which the course of

action it advocated could confer benefit on the entire polis. Emanating out of a link between legein and phronein, political discourse became that discourse which could capture eloquently, address persuasively, and resolve symbolically the irresolutions that a given issue created for the Athenians.

As with the aesthetic, the political also acquired an element of leisure, a constituent part absent from the history of political oratory.[20] Now attached to general questions and broad issues, political discourse could assume the new role of addressing general issues concerning the future of the polis, while letting the assembly continue with its familiar role of settling issues through policy.[21] Divorced from political oratory in the assembly, political discourse did not merely take up a new subject matter but was also subjected to a new conception of time. Questions concerning the future direction of the polis, but detached from the pressures of policy making, could now be raised and discussed differently. There was time now to consider options carefully and weigh alternatives thoughtfully. Public orators could be given the leisure to think through implications and consequences, factoring in the likelihood of unanticipated circumstances and unexpected situations. In short, there was time now to proceed cautiously and prudentially.

By linking legein and phronein Isocrates managed, in effect, to retard the process of political deliberation. Under his direction political deliberation—now reconceived as public deliberation—became hospitable to reflection and amenable to circumspection. And we might better be able to understand why Isocrates chose the name of philosophy for his educational program when we consider the viable role that reflection, circumspection, and even refutation played in the deliberating process as he conceived it. For political discourse, once providing an exclusive site for the workings of persuasion, now became part of a process wide enough to include into its very texture the workings of a thinking mind: "the same arguments which we use in persuading others when we speak in public, we employ also when we deliberate in our own thoughts; and, while we call eloquent those who are able to speak before a crowd, we regard as sage those who most skilfully debate their problems in their own minds" (περὶ τῶν πραγμάτων διαλεχθῶσιν) (*Antidosis* 256). Public deliberation, in its widest possible procedure and in its most leisurely conduct, has room now to take on its texture and appropriate and benefit from the method of dialectic. It is with this kind of political discourse in mind that Isocrates could proclaim his version of rhetoric to be eloquence and wisdom in one: "the power to speak well (*legein*) is taken as the surest index of a sound understanding (*phronein*)" (*Nicocles* 7, *Antidosis* 255).

Finally, the new spaciousness of public deliberation, produced by the link of legein to phronein and made reverberant by its contact with a new conception of time, became affable to ethical considerations. The effort to address broad questions regarding the future direction of the polis would go unheeded unless the caution and the thoughtfulness expended on political options were somehow extended to include considerations about ethical choices and moral ends. Indeed Isocrates' version of public deliberation approached questions about the general direction of the polis not merely as a political issue but as an ethico-political concern. The sizing up of the general predicament of the polis opened up questions not only about what was possible for the polis but also about what was good for the polis. Away from the assembly there was time to determine what would be a desirable direction for the polis to take and also whether the direction proposed or the course of action advocated would be consistent with the values of the polis. For Isocrates, as the *Panegyricus* demonstrates, a general proposal for action would be unimaginable if the political inquiry conducted did not also include an ethical inquiry, or if the proposal to action did not also clarify the values affirmed by that action. In his call for a clear relation between political advocacy and ethical affirmation, Isocrates had history on his side. An example is the Mytilinean expedition. This was a nightmarish event created by a public vote in the assembly to punish the Mytilineans for dishonoring their contract with the Athenian empire by sending the Athenian fleet to destroy them followed by a reversal of the decision the next day and another trireme being sent almost too late to catch up with the fleet. This event is a historical reminder of how little time moral considerations took up in the assembly. The burden in the Athenians' conscience, which could only have been captured by Thucydides' pen, confirms the existence of the need Isocrates sought to meet by conceiving deliberation as an ethico-political practice, an interaction of values and courses of action. In the context of deliberation as a public enterprise, there is time to propose and to revoke, to make ends explicit and to reserve the right to change one's mind. In such deliberation legein and phronein meet each other in a way that the welfare of the polis becomes the site of an inquiry into values and action, and an examination into the good and the possible.

III

Before turning to examine Isocrates' notion of public deliberation, however, we must defend the argument that has been advanced all along—that the link between legein and phronein effected by Isocrates was an indissoluble one. The need for such a defense is created by Isocrates' own discussion about the incommensurability of aesthetic and didactic ends. Indeed, near the end of *To Nicocles*, an oration composed by inartistically stringing together a series of maxims, Isocrates concedes the point that speeches giving advice could not also be pleasurable, or that admonitory discourses could not also be shaped artistically. Orators wishing to give advice, he argues, are constrained by the necessity to deploy the familiar and the commonsensical for the purpose of dissuading audiences from actual or potential mistakes—a constraint that leads orators away from the artistic and the pleasurable: "In discourses of this sort," he remarks, orators cannot afford to "seek novelties, for in these discourses it is not possible to say what is paradoxical or incredible or outside the circle of accepted belief" (41). All one can do, he continues, is repeat what others have already said, namely, "collect the greatest number of ideas scattered among the thoughts of all the rest and present them in the best form" (41). Yet, he is quick to point out, audiences derive no pleasure from hearing the familiar and find no delight in being told what to do, even though the counsel they receive may be useful. In his words, "while all men think that those compositions . . . are the most useful which counsel us how to live, yet it is certainly not to them that they listen with greatest pleasure" (42). "How, then," he asks in resignation, "can one advise or teach or say anything of profit and yet please such people?" (46).

Neither the weight of this question nor the burden of the dilemma it poses for Isocrates can be grasped in the isolated context of this brief discussion in *To Nicocles*. For the sharp contrast drawn here, between the impulse to please and the impulse to advise, plays into the persona Isocrates is creating for himself in this text—the type of adviser to the king who, committed to giving the best advice, speaks without regard to what the interlocutor wishes to hear: "it is evident that those who desire to command the attention of their hearers must abstain from admonition and advice, and must say the kinds of things which they see are most pleasing to the crowd" (49). Similarly, the notion of the incommensurability of admonition and delight plays also into Isocrates' strategy to concede the inartistic character of this particular oration. Hence the repeated plea made to the reader not to judge a selection of maxims by the standard of an artistic composition, or the nature of the advice given by the standard of pleasure: "you ought not to judge what things are worthy or what men are wise by the standard of pleasure, but to appraise them in the light of conduct that is useful" (50).

Outside this oration, Isocrates' discussion about the incommensurable character of advice and pleasure makes little sense. For in many of his writings Isocrates sets out to accomplish precisely the very goal that in *To Nicocles* is said to be implausible: to counsel his auditors in a manner that would also delight them, and to give them advice in a way that would also bring them pleasure. The retrospective remarks he makes in the *Anti-*

dosis about his previous writings demonstrate that his effort to combine counsel with delight has been both an ongoing and a self-conscious aim. In past orations he had sought, he argues in the *Antidosis,* not only to offer important advice on the affairs of the state but also to delight the Athenians: "[I] have chosen rather to write discourses, not for private disputes, but which deal with the world of Hellas, with affairs of state, and are appropriate to be delivered at the Pan-Hellenic assemblies—discourses which, as everyone will agree, are more akin to works composed in rhythm and set to music than to the speeches which are made in court" (46). The affinity between his own discourses and "works composed in rhythm" is drawn not only in terms of linking together counsel and delight, but also in terms of connecting prose with poetry: "For they set forth facts in a style more imaginative and more ornate; they employ thoughts which are more lofty and more original, and, besides, they use throughout figures of speech in greater number and of more striking character" (47). The conclusion Isocrates draws from this discussion contradicts the claim he had earlier made concerning the incommensurability of counsel and delight. For what he expresses at present is the belief that his past orations had successfully created a type of prose that offers fruitful counsel at the same time that it produces delight, a delight no less pleasurable than that associated with poetry: "All men take as much pleasure in listening to this kind of prose as in listening to poetry" (47).

It is unfortunate that Isocrates never fulfilled the promise he made in the *Panathenaicus* to write a treatise on the poets and to expound his views on poetry as well as poetry's relation to his rhetorical training (25). Had such a treatise been written, it would have undoubtedly given us a better grasp of the precise relationship he had attempted to establish between admonitory and pleasurable ends, and perhaps a clearer understanding of the more general link he had sought to forge between *legein* and *phronein*. In the absence of such a treatise, it is tempting to keep counsel and delight apart and, following Isocrates' own cue from *To Nicocles,* look to his orations as works born out of either one or the other impulse. This is precisely what Gunther Heilbrunn has done in a recent essay that, taking counsel and pleasure to be mutually exclusive impulses, divides Isocrates' major writings into two distinct groups—orations driven by the useful or the pleasurable, the sober or the seductive. On the one side of this divide, Heilbrunn places the Panhellenic orations, the *Helen,* the *Panegyricus,* the *Panathenaicus*—speeches advocating war, praisingAthens after the manner of poets/eulogists, claiming artistic innovation, employing mythical material, and aiming at pleasing auditors. On the other side, there are the civic orations, the *Areopagiticus* and *On the Peace,* speeches advocating civic reform and admonishing Athens, orations claiming no artistic innovation, repeating the tradition of gnomic poets and the persuasive uses of commonplace maxims, and aiming at implanting moderation and self-restraint.

The sharp contrast drawn above between the useful and the pleasurable cannot explain Isocrates' desire to assign to his orations, as we have seen, the double aim of producing delight in listeners and of offering advice to them. Nor can it explain why Isocrates regards the process of producing pleasure in hearers as an integral part of his rhetorical education, an instruction that does not stop with politically useful compositions but goes on to cover aesthetic matters as well by teaching students how "to adorn the whole speech with striking thoughts and to clothe it in flowing and melodious phrase" (*Against the Sophists* 16). Finally, it cannot account for the mission he assigned to himself when he undertook to write the *Evagoras*—to compose an encomium of the dead king that would not only delight his surviving son and new king but also counsel him how to live his life.

Indeed, in the *Evagoras* Isocrates complicates the sharp contrast he had previously maintained between useful and delightful discourses as well as the stark opposition he had drawn between the impulse to advise and the impulse to please. In this oration delight appears to be a prerequisite of advice, and pleasure emerges as a required condition for a successful guidance and admonition. "For we exhort young men to the study of philosophy," he exclaims near the end of the oration, "by praising others in order that they, emulating those who are eulogized, may desire to adopt the same pursuits, but I appeal to you and yours, using as examples not aliens, but members of your own family, and I counsel you to devote your attention to this, that you may not be surpassed in either word or deed by any of the Hellenes" (77). The extent to which Nicocles will heed Isocrates' advice and follow on his father's footsteps seems to be directly analogous to the delight Nicocles will receive from the portrait of his father as it is drawn by the encomiast's pen. Having reconceived delight and counsel as mutually dependent impulses, Isocrates can now ascertain the use value behind his own pleasurable discourse. Throughout the eulogy of Evagoras he has sought, he tells Nicocles, "to speak and to write in such fashion as may be likely to incite you to strive eagerly after those things which even now you do in fact desire" (80). The pleasure produced through discourse, earlier dismissed as useless activity and without benefit to auditors, is now given an indispensable part in the larger process of guiding audiences successfully: "I have undertaken to write this discourse," he tells Nicocles, "because I believed that for you, for your children, and for all the other descendants of Evagoras, it would be by far the best incentive, if someone should assemble his achievements, give them verbal adornment, and submit them to you for your contemplation and study" (76).

In *To Nicocles* Isocrates had spoken about the poetic tradition in terms of two mutually exclusive strands. On the one hand, there is Homer and the tragedians, who delighted audiences by deploying mythic material and produced pleasure by appealing to the senses: "Homer has dressed the contests and battles of the demigods in myths, while the tragic poets have rendered the myths in the form of contests and action, so that they are presented, not to our ears alone, but to our eyes as well" (49). On the other hand, there is the strand of the gnomic poets, Hesiod and Theognis, who, even though recognized as by far "the best counsellors for human conduct" (43), remained largely unread, since their sober imitation of the real produces no pleasure, and since most people "would lend a readier ear to the cheapest comedy" than listen to the maxims of these "leading poets" (44). In the *Evagoras* Isocrates abandons this reductive scheme and redefines his relation to the poetic tradition by positioning himself in the aftermath of such encomiasts as Pindar and Bacchylides and by seeing himself as their prosaic counterpart. The task he is presently undertaking—"to eulogize in prose the virtues of a man" (8)—is without precedent, he declares in the opening of the *Evagoras*. Even though orators before him had left those types of undertakings to the poets, he remarks, he will nevertheless "make the effort and see if it will be possible in prose to eulogize good men in no worse fashion than their encomiasts do who employ song and verse" (11).

Thus redefining his relation to the tradition of poetry, Isocrates accepts the poetic function of *psychagogein* (guiding souls) as part and parcel of his oratorical enterprise. In *To Nicocles* the power to charm and seduce audiences was relegated to the domain of poetry, linked to the production of pleasure, and completely disassociated from admonition and advice (49). In the *Evagoras* this same power is once again considered to be the poets' property: "by the very spell of their rhythm and harmony they bewitch their listeners" (ψυχαγωγοῦσι τοὺς ἀκούοντας) (10). But in the context of this eulogy, and in view of this encomiastic undertaking, the power to charm and seduce audiences can be claimed by orators as well.[22] Indeed, Isocrates claims to be a formidable rival to the poets in that he is able to produce a prosaic encomium no less pleasurable than theirs. More importantly, he rivals his encomiastic predecessors in having used his art with words to create a powerful portrait that would act as an incentive to audiences to accept guidance and advice (76).[23] The extent to which Nicocles stands to follow the orator's advice is made to depend entirely on the power of the orator to produce a seductive portrait of Evagoras.

Elsewhere I have shown that Isocrates' power with encomiastic praise stems from his capacity to follow the poetic tradition of the genre and, at the same time, to adapt the genre's formal requirements to the demands of giving political advice in his day.[24] Here the stress is on the indissolubly double character of Isocrates' rhetoric, with the *Evagoras* submitted as a case in point, an example of the inextricable link he was able to forge between eloquence and reflection. In the *Evagoras* the artistic display of Evagoras' deeds was given the function of guiding Nicocles' conduct; the orator's display of his art was put to the task of giving advice to a ruler; and the form of self-display (*epideixis*) was given the new mission of making itself responsive to the needs of the polis. Understood in this light, the *Evagoras* exemplifies the type of oratory Isocrates held in highest regard and felt most certain he had produced in at least one instance—his *Panegyricus:* "I have singled out as the highest kind of oratory that which deals with the greatest affairs and, while best displaying the ability of those who speak, brings most profit to those who hear; and this oration is of that character" (4).

Chapter Five

Public Deliberation
Panegyricus

Purporting to be addressing a Panhellenic festival, Isocrates opens the *Panegyricus* by stating directly the course of action he is advocating for the Hellenes: "I have come before you to give my counsels on the war against the barbarians and on concord among ourselves" (3). Having stated his proposal, he acknowledges that it is not a new one and that many others before him had also addressed the prospect of a united Hellenic expedition against Asia: "but since oratory is of such a nature that it is possible to discourse on the same subject matter in many different ways," he argues, "it follows that one must not shun the subjects upon which others have spoken before, but must try to speak better than they" (8). Even though the general proposal has been made before, he promises to surpass his predecessors through his unique treatment of it: "I hope to rise so far superior to them that it will seem as if no word had ever been spoken by my rivals upon this subject" (4).

Isocrates does not elaborate on his unique approach to this old theme, a theme that his reported teacher, Gorgias, had also addressed at the Panhellenic festival at Olympia in 408. He merely insinuates that his oration will be the kind one would expect to hear from a person blessed with practical wisdom: "For the deeds of the past are, indeed, an inheritance common to us all; but the ability to make proper use of them at the appropriate time, to conceive the right sentiments about them in each instance, and to set them forth in finished phrase, is the peculiar gift of the wise, *eu phronounton*" (9). Isocrates poses himself to the Athenians, and perhaps to the Greeks, as the wise counselor that Thucydides mentioned. I say "to the Athenians" rather than "to the Greeks" because it is doubtful that the oration was ever intended to be delivered at a festival, given its length.[1] But there is no doubt that it was widely circulated among the Athenian intellectuals and, as its popularity suggests, must have been well known by a good portion of a nonreading public as well.[2] And it is also possible that Isocrates might have expected his oration to reach some non-Athenians as well.

Given the time it took Isocrates to complete it, and the fame it brought to him among his contemporaries, the *Panegyricus* undoubtedly made an important sourcebook to students training in rhetoric. And even though we have no evidence of how exactly Isocrates used his orations to instruct his students, we can nevertheless derive some benefit from entertaining the perspective of pedagogy and from looking at the *Panegyricus* from the point of view of the contributions it could have made to their training in rhetorical education. What such a perspective makes immediately apparent is the possibility that, of all Isocrates' works, the *Panegyricus* would have been the text most appropriate to train students in public deliberation and to provide satisfactory answers to the question most politicians-to-be would have wanted to raise, namely, how does one go about deliberating?

And if this line of reasoning is extended one step further, then Isocrates' remark about wisdom acquires an added significance, a pertinence to public deliberation that otherwise would go unnoticed and remain undetected behind the prominent sense of the remark as a gesture of self-praise. It may very well be, therefore, that the deliberative process unfolding in the pages of the *Panegyricus* not only demonstrates Isocrates' unique take on deliberating this particular subject but also gives an example of what public deliberation would look like were it to issue from an orator possessing practical wisdom. Viewing the *Panegyricus* as a result of practical wisdom allows us to give substance to Isocrates' claims that he could teach his students how to deliberate wisely and make them proficient in the art of rhetoric as he conceived it, i.e., as a blending of legein and phronein.

Before beginning such an inquiry, it should be pointed out that the translations of Isocrates' terms such as *phronein* and *phronesis* are highly irregular. Most of the time Norlin and Van Hook translate *phronesis* as "practical wisdom" in contradistinction to "philosophical wisdom" or *sophia*. As we consult various passages that include these terms, however, we should keep in mind that the translation will not always be consistent. Even though this poses some difficulties, it is necessary; for the distinction between philosophical and practical wisdom is an Aristotelian distinction, and we cannot assume that Isocrates' use of these terms will always coincide with Aristotle's.[3] In Isocrates' case, we can only proceed contextually.

There is little doubt that in the context of public deliberation, whether he uses *sophia* or *phronesis*, Isocrates is in either case suggesting the kind of insight or judgment necessary for orators to deal with the uncertainties of the deliberating situation. For any advocacy of action involves the future, and the course of action endorsed as the best case scenario is a mere guess until the events unfolding in the future determine whether the action taken was in fact correct or incorrect and whether the guess made was lucky or unfortunate. Because deliberation involves uncertainty, correct insight and good judgment are bound to remain within the province of luck (*ty-che*).[4] And even though Isocrates claims to improve orators' insight and judgment with deliberation, he is well aware that oftentimes luck will outdo wisdom: "I know that in times when your city deliberates on matters of the greatest import those who are reputed to be the wisest (*arista phronein*) sometimes miss the expedient course of action, whereas now and then some chance person from the ranks of men who are deemed of no account and are regarded with contempt hits upon (*tychon*) the right course" (*Panathenaicus*, 248).

Under his direction the study of *phronein* reduces the element of chance and minimizes the possibility of error. As he puts it in the *Antidosis*, "men who have been gifted with eloquence by nature and by fortune, are governed in what they say by chance (*tyche*), and not by any standard of what is best, whereas those who have gained this power by the study of philosophy and by the exercise of reason never speak without weighing their words, and so are less often in error as to a course of action" (292). As we turn to the deliberative process in the *Panegyricus* and examine how good judgments are made, we will also be looking at Isocrates' claim that he can in fact turn opinion into wisdom, *doxa* into *phronesis*. For this was the crux of Isocrates' pedagogical promise: "I hold that man to be wise (*sophos*) who is able by his powers of conjecture (*doxa*) to arrive generally at the best course, and I hold that man to be a philosopher who occupies himself with the studies from which he will most quickly gain that kind of insight (*phronesis*)" (*Antidosis* 271).

I

In the *Panegyricus* deliberation unfolds by means of an ethico-political inquiry, an inquiry into the good and the possible for the polis. Isocrates defends the proposal for Hellenes to unite and undertake an expedition against Asia as a sound decision for Athens, a good ethical and political choice. The work offers us occasion to examine the procedures by which good judgments of value are made and to compare these with procedures by which good judgments of action are made. As we undertake this examination, it is important to point out that our focus on good judgment requires us to bracket good expression, and our consideration of practical wisdom requires us to suspend our attention to artistic eloquence. But as we have seen in the previous chapter, *phronein* and *legein* are inseparable for Isocrates, two inextricably connected components of one and the same art. We separate the two, therefore, only for the purposes of analysis, keeping in mind throughout that the ethically good and the politically possible are connected for Isocrates not only pragmatically—through the benefit that good judgment confers on the polis—but also artistically—through the display good judgment makes of the orator's ability to deliberate.

Isocrates reminds us of this right from the start. For as he undertakes the task of defending the proposal as the result of good judgment, he frames his own inquiry within the following definition of oratory: "I have singled out as the highest kind of oratory that which deals with the greatest affairs and, while best displaying (*epideiknyousi*) the ability of those who speak, brings most profit to those who hear; and this oration is of that character" (4–5). The *Panegyricus* is a display of Isocrates' judgments on ethical and political choices. And as display, as a piece of *epideixis*, it can be expected to perform artistically the very counsel Isocrates offers to the Athenians. We will return to this thought following our analysis—the thought, in other words, that public deliberation is, for Isocrates, the rhetorical performance of procedures by which good judgments of ethical and political choices are made.

As a way of distinguishing his oration from others, who had proposed a similar course of action, Isocrates calls attention to his unique point of departure, a historical account of Athens from its mythical origins to present times. Earlier orators, he remarks, "do speak the truth, but they do not start at the point from which they could best bring these things to pass" (15). Only this account, Isocrates argues, will persuade Athenians and Lacedaemonians alike that the leadership for such an expedition ought to be shared equally by both. And unless the question of leadership is resolved, the general proposal will continue to remain a topic for deliberation without ever turning to policy. In defense of the long mythical-historical narrative he is about to recount, he says: "So, then, the other speakers also should have made this their starting-point and should not have given advice on matters about which we agree before instructing us on the points about which we disagree" (19). A look into the past is necessary if the proposal is to resolve satisfactorily issues of disagreement. For it is only through the past that judgments informing courses of action at present may be best defended: "the farther back into the past we go in our examination of both [Athenian and Lacedaemonian] titles to leadership, the farther behind shall we leave those who dispute our claims" (22).

According to Isocrates, then, good judgments of action are reached by an interplay of the general character of past cases and the particular character of present instances. Athens' claim to hegemony in the present is illuminated by past cases, mythical and historical moments when Athens assumed the position of leadership and guided all of Hellas to a better place. The *Panegyricus* offers a variety of such moments, a multiplicity of fictional and factual histories. Thus, there is the agricultural story,

Demeter's gift of "the fruits of the earth" and Athens' initiative in instructing the rest of the Hellenes "in their uses, their cultivation, and the benefits derived from them" (28–29); the story of the Ionic migration and the leading role Athens played in extending the boundaries of Hellas (34–37); the story of laws and Athens' pioneering example with giving order to her own house (38–40); the stories of commerce, festivals, and arts along with the exchanges and interactions among the Hellenes each one of these made possible (41–50); the story of the Trojan War and the story of the Seven Against Thebes, along with Athens' commitment to the allies and her beneficence to the oppressed city-states (54–67); and finally, the culminating moment of the history of the Persian invasion against Greece at the turn of the fifth century (68–98).

"Who then should have the hegemony," Isocrates asks after recounting these past cases of Athenian leadership, "when a campaign against the barbarians is in prospect?" Yet, even though the force of his lengthy narrative rests on historical precedent and seems to endorse repetition of the past in the present, a closer look at the historical cases narrated reveals that Isocrates uses the past as guide to rather than as model for the present. The past cannot be repeated in the present, and Isocrates knows it.[5] What has intervened in between the past and the present, and what, as a result, renders the general case inapplicable to the present situation, is the ruthless conduct of the Athenian Empire. An argument for repetition would have no persuasive force with the allies, for whom a call for Athenian hegemony could only have meant an invitation to an Athenian tyranny.

The prolonged attention Isocrates devotes to the period of Athens' peak following the Persian Wars, along with the sustained defense he offers of the empire's conduct (100–137), shows cognizance of the unique situation Athens faces at this time. Without the military might it once commanded, Athenian hegemony must rely on the support and cooperation of city-states whose trust it no longer has.[6] And it is this unique predicament of present Athens that shapes Isocrates' accounts of past Athenian leadership. The mythical and historical narratives he recounts are not designed to invoke the authority of precedents as much as they are intended to redefine hegemony in ways that would eradicate, as much as possible, all connotations of imperialism and tyranny that the notion of Athenian hegemony would be certain to stir in the allied city-states.[7]

And it is this double effort to appeal to past cases of hegemony and, at the same time, to redefine hegemony that we have already designated as an interplay in the deliberative process between past cases and present situations, a sign of practical wisdom at work. The interplay itself becomes most evident when we watch Isocrates' narratives of past cases of leadership unfold by dividing the known world in spatial terms and by keeping this spatial division between Hellenes and barbarians intact, as a division of the "we" from the "they."

While the merits of the expedition against Asia are defended on various grounds, all points argued and all appeals made are informed by the demarcation that has already taken place in narrative accounts, and Athenian leadership is now extolled in terms of defending the sacred grounds of Hellas from an invasion of the protruding other and now lauded in terms of expanding the boundaries past the enemy lines and giving the Hellenes the land they need and the territory they deserve. Now investing the barbarian with the power to annihilate the city-states' right to govern themselves, now with the power to raise obstacles to the city-states' freedom to pursue their prosperity, Isocrates portrays the Persians as inextricably involved with Greek autonomy and freedom—the two principles on which the very identity of every Hellenic city-state was based.[8]

A similar interplay of past cases and present situation is evident in Isocrates' construction of the "we." The sharp division that exists among city-states and the keen animosity that characterizes their relations can be grasped as an alliance only by the mediating agency of a narrative account that represents past events by accentuating similarities and minimizing differences. And while the positing of the barbarian other is meant to serve precisely the function of consolidating diverse city-states into an integrated "we," Isocrates takes a step further and helps the process of consolidation along by means of a narrative whose very mission seems to be none other than to construct unity out of division. Indeed, Athens' relation to Sparta is actively constructed under the process of a consolidation. At the opening of the *Panegyricus* the Lacedaemonians are portrayed as the sole opponents to shared leadership and the unreasonable supporters of "the false doctrine that leadership is theirs by ancestral right" (18). If he cannot persuade the Greeks to implement his proposal, Isocrates remarks, he must at least expose those who are to blame and "show who they are that stand in the way of the happiness of the Hellenes" (20). During the war against the Thebans, Athenians are shown to have defended the cause of the sons of Heracles and to have helped them establish themselves in the region of Lacedaemon. But these benefits were eventually forgotten, and the Lacedaemonians prove themselves unworthy of the kindness shown to them by the Athenians: "These benefits they should have held in grateful remembrance, and should never have invaded this land from which they set out and acquired so great prosperity, nor have placed in peril the city which had imperiled herself for the sons of Heracles" (62).

In the account of the Persian Wars, however, the terms of the relationship between Athens and Sparta undergo radical change. The battles at Marathon and Thermopylae are presented not merely as brave efforts to stop the oncoming enemy but as reliable indexes of selfless attempts to defend the freedom of the entire Hellas. The Athenians and Lacedaemonians are portrayed as eagerly running to the rescue of all other city-states and zealously competing against each other for who would place the Hellenes under the greatest obligation (73). In view of the common threat, the relationship between Athens and Sparta is redefined from animosity to rivalry and from hostility to a competition for the prize of general safety: "Now while our forefathers and the Lacedaemonians were always emulous of each other, yet during that time their rivalry was for the noblest ends; they did not look upon each other as enemies but as competitors . . . and their rivalry with each other was solely to see which of them should bring [the Hellenes' safety] about" (85).

This gesture of placing the two archenemies of Hellas under a common cause and forging unity out of division is only one instance of a larger consolidating process undertaken by and put into effect through the narrative progression. As the narrative unfolds, terms lose their specificity and signifiers become unattached from their ordinary context-specific meaning. One such signifier is the term *fatherland* (*patris*), a term ordinarily attached to and drawing its signification from the specific city of one's origins.[9] Consistent with ordinary language use of the times, Isocrates starts his narrative account by praising Athens as the Athenians' home, "at once nurse and fatherland (*patrida*) and mother" (25). One's fatherland cannot be different from one's polis. But the story of Athenian hegemony is the story of Athenian beneficence, an altruistic defense of common benefits and a selfless fight for common salvation. It is the story of a citizenly conduct which, initiated by the leaders, becomes contagious for the rest. As a result, one's fatherland no longer coincides with but rather exceeds one's polis: "and, while they regarded their home cities (*poleis*) as their several places of abode, yet they considered Hellas to be their common fatherland" (κοινὴν δὲ πατρίδα τὴν Ἑλλάδα νομίζοντες εἶναι) (81).

I have alluded to Isocrates' deliberation in the *Panegyricus* as an instance of practical wisdom at work. And so far, I have attempted to capture the operations of practical wisdom as an interplay between past cases and present situations. The advocacy for Athenian hegemony is supported through past cases; yet the idiosyncrasy of the present situation prevents Isocrates from understanding past cases as anything more than a flexible guide. Recognizing the uniqueness of the present situation, Isocrates respects the present's resilience to the past and permits the past case to illuminate the present moment only as much as he allows the present to illuminate the past. Wise deliberation unfolds by means of a process according to which the general illuminates the particular and the particular illuminates the general. And this interplay between the general and the particular provides a context that guides the deliberating orator to read the new situation wisely and reach a prudent decision—not only as concerns political choices but also as regards ethical choices.

The recounting of past instances of Athenian hegemony, we saw, was used by Isocrates in order to invoke Athens' defense of the principles of autonomy and safety for all allied city-states. And Isocrates continues to invoke these principles even in that section in which he discusses the imperialistic conduct of past Athens. Yet the inquiry he undertakes next, the lengthy examination of the great king's successful activities and interventions within Greek affairs, leads to a grim portrait of a general disorder and shared devastation for the entire Hellas. The people have experienced, Isocrates cries out, "every form of horror; for many as are the ills which are incident to the nature of man, we have ourselves invented more than those which necessity lays upon us, by engendering wars and factions among ourselves; and, in consequence, some are being put to death contrary to law in their own countries, others are wandering with their women and children in strange lands, and many, compelled through lack of the necessities of life to enlist in foreign armies, are being slain, fighting for their foes against their friends" (167–68). Responsibility for the rising power of the king and the continued devastation of Hellas belongs to all Greeks, not just the Athenians: "And all this has come about by reason of our own folly, not because of his power" (137). For all share alike in a strife they have equally created, and with consequences so inhumane that even the barbarians would want to escape: "we should be in utmost dread," Isocrates laments, "of that time when the conflicting interests of the barbarians are settled and are governed by a single purpose, while we continue to be, as now, hostile to each other" (138). Given this common condition, the initial call for Athenian hegemony becomes superseded by a call for unity: "it is much more glorious to fight against the King for his empire than to contend against each other for the hegemony" (166).

The topic of poverty shifts Isocrates' discourse from praise (Athens) and blame (Sparta) and turns the focus toward their common condition of misery and their shared predicament of mistrust. Poverty, he remarks, "breaks up friendships, perverts the affections of kindred into enmity, and plunges the whole world into war and strife" (174). Should economic necessities be left unremedied, no genuine ties will ever be possible for the Greeks: "For as matters now stand, it is in vain that we make our treaties of peace; for we do not settle our wars, but only postpone them and wait for the opportune moment when we shall have the power to inflict some irreparable disaster upon each other" (172). In this manner, the values associated with hegemony (power and safety) take second seat to values associated with unity (cooperation, trust, and friendship). And the present predicament of Greece (division, strife, mistrust) gives an un-precedented urgency to the old theme of Panhellenism. This time around, the cry for Panhellenism issues not from a single city-state's drive to con-quer[10] but from a collectivity bound together in a common fate and a shared destiny, a fate forged out of mutual economic conditions and a destiny created by a joint desire for genuine ties: "It is not possible for us to cement an enduring peace unless we join together in a war against the barbarians, nor for the Hellenes to attain to concord until we wrest our material advantages from one and the same source and wage our wars against one and the same enemy" (173). Only then, he goes on, "we shall enjoy a spirit of concord, and the good will which we shall feel towards each other will be genuine" (174).

As with action, therefore, so with values; as with political choices, ethi-cal choices are made by an interplay of the general and the particular. The wise orator must be prepared to witness the integrity of the concrete par-ticular and understand the unique ethical demands it makes. Past cases entail moral precepts that render the present instance morally intelligible only in part, and the orator must be prepared to revise the moral frame-work brought onto the particular. In the *Panegyricus*, then, procedures by which good judgments of value are made coincide with procedures by which good judgments of action are made. With choices of action as with choices of value, practical wisdom guides the orator cognitively and mor-ally in a similar manner and directs the orator's inquiry into the ethically good and the politically possible down the same path. Yet, where does the ability to read the particular correctly come from? What regulates the in-terplay of the general and the particular in political and ethical choice?

II

In the *Antidosis* experience is a crucial prerequisite of practical wisdom. In a passage in which he openly defines his profession, Isocrates makes the following remark: "It remains to tell you about 'wisdom' and 'philosophy' (*sophia kai philosophia*). . . . My view of this question is, as it happens, very simple. For since it is not in the nature of man to attain a science (*episteme*) by the possession of which we can know positively what we should do or what we should say, in the next resort I hold that man to be wise (*sophos*) who is able by his powers of conjecture (*doxa*) to arrive generally at the best course, and I hold that man to be a philosopher who occupies himself with the studies from which he will most quickly gain that kind of insight, *phronesin*" (270–71). Because deliberation deals with the future and ren-ders definite judgments on situations that present themselves with uncer-tainty and ambivalence, human opinion or conjecture (doxa) is the only guide to making judgments. And since doxa belongs to the province of luck (tyche), experience is the only resource humans have to turn doxa from a whimsical to an insightful conjecture. Experience wrests doxa from tyche and turns it into judgment.[11]

Experience (*empeiria*) is also one of the three requisites to Isocrates' rhetorical education, the other two being natural talent with speaking (physis) and knowledge of the art (*paideusis*). Students can expect to excel in rhetoric if they have a natural aptitude, if they learn the knowledges of the art, and if they "become versed and practiced in the use and application of their art" (γυμνασθῆναι περὶ τὴν χρείαν καὶ τὴν ἐμπειρίαν αὐτῶν) (187). And while physis and paideusis pertain either to student or teacher, experience involves both in a continual training: "In this process, master and pupil each has his place; no one but the pupil can furnish the necessary capacity; no one but the master, the ability to impart knowledge; while both have a part in the exercises of practical application" (ἐμπειρίαν γυμνάσιον) (188).

Isocrates assigns the least importance to learning, since acquisition of knowledge does not amount to anything much if it remains unsupported by natural talent or experience (192). And while he considers the latter two to be equally important (189–91), he does associate natural talent with luck and the insight that results from one's natural make-up with an ability that can only be accidental. Like those who have inherited a fortune from their parents, innately eloquent speakers, he argues, do not get much credit: "And rightly so; for it is well that in all activities, and most of all in the art of speaking, credit is won, not by gifts of fortune, but by efforts of study. For men who have been gifted with eloquence by nature and by fortune (*physei kai tyche*), are governed in what they say by chance (ὅπως ἂν τύχωσιν), and not by any standard of what is best, whereas those who have gained this power by the study of philosophy and by the exercise of reason (*logismo*) never speak without weighing their words, and so are less often in error as to a course of action" (292). Thus, even though natural talent may be the most important asset for eloquence, it cannot yield the kind of discerning ability that deliberation demands and practical wisdom requires.

Instead, it is practice and experience that sharpen the reasoning process and develop good insight and sound judgment. This is why teachers, Isocrates insists, must require students "to combine in practice the particular things which they have learned"; for only those "who most apply their minds to [the occasions] and are able to discern the consequences which for the most part grow out of them, will most often meet these occasions in the right way" (184). Yet experience does not merely sharpen intellectual faculties; it additionally cultivates and improves the capacity to imagine. Learning how to apply one's knowledge of the art to living situations is most difficult and most arduous. The demands of application, Isocrates underscores, "are the task of a vigorous and imaginative mind" (ψυχῆς δοξαστικῆς ἔργον εἶναι) (*Sophists* 17).

Experience wrests doxa from tyche, then, by guiding doxa toward practical wisdom, that is, toward the place where intellect and imagination, reason and emotion intersect. Recognizing that wise deliberation is the outcome of a long experience with life, Isocrates presents the *Panegyricus* as an oration informed by his lifelong experience. "I [will] speak," he announces to his listeners, "in a manner worthy of my subject and of my reputation and of the time which I have spent—not merely the hours which have been devoted to my speech but also all the years which I have lived" (14).

Our analysis of the *Panegyricus* as an index of deliberation informed by practical wisdom would not be complete unless the role that experience plays in deliberation is also shown; for experience guides the deliberating agent's ability to respond to situations cognitively and passionately, intellectually and emotionally. In situations requiring political and ethical choices, experience provides an invaluable resource of commitments sustained over the span of many years by reason and passion alike. Good judgments, therefore, cannot be made without the insight gained through experience or the guidance that comes from a lifelong interplay of intellectual perception and emotional response.

We have seen that Isocrates provides some good reasons in defense of an expedition against Asia. In addition to these, he does not neglect to make some sound military arguments. "So it seems to me that the motives which summon us to enter upon a war against them are many indeed; but chief among them is the present opportunity (ὁ παρὼν καιρός), which we must not throw away; for it is disgraceful to neglect a chance when it is present and regret it when it is past" (160). Taking this as an opportunity to display his knowledge of foreign matters, he offers a detailed analysis of the great king's warring operations, the various fronts he is forced to divide his army into, and the weakness that results from such a division. Experience dictates, he argues, that one must strike first, before the enemy has the time to organize, consolidate, and turn all his power toward Greece. "Therefore," he concludes, "we must be quick and not waste time, in order that we may not repeat the experience of our fathers" (164).

Yet Isocrates also shows that a person of experience does not bring to a situation intelligence alone, but rather responds to it with passion as well. In the *Panegyricus* intellectual and emotional responses to the Panhellenic proposal coincide, as Isocrates allows his deliberation to be informed by desires and his desires to be guided by deliberation. Thus, in addition to a military target, the Persians also become the object of vengeance for the

Greeks, who desire to avenge the barbaric activities at Ion of "rifling even the images and temples of the gods, and burning them to the ground" (155); the object of just punishment, for those who desire justice in view of all the injustices and injuries done to the Greeks (183); and the object of a religious duty, for those who "desire to serve their gods" (184). Guided by deliberation through sound military reasons, the combined desires for vengeance, justice, and reverence guide deliberation, in turn, to a non-military campaign: "it will be more like a sacred mission than a military expedition" (182). Reason and desire coordinate to demonstrate to audiences the kind of situation they are dealing with, and to guide judgment to the same place. "Do not the Persians," Isocrates asks, "fulfill all these conditions?" (184).

Desire guides reason in the situation of choice by marking what is to be pursued and what is to be avoided. And we have seen that marking take place throughout the *Panegyricus*, as the action to be taken is also shown to be at once a destination to and a departure from unity and division, friendship and strife, prosperity and poverty, vengeance and indignation. And it is this marking of what is to be pursued and avoided through desire, and the action desire guides to, that makes up one of the two final images Isocrates leaves his audience with: "try to picture to yourselves what vast prosperity we should attain if we should turn the war which now involves ourselves against the peoples of the continent, and bring the prosperity of Asia across to Europe" (187). Yet the role of desire in deliberation is not just motivational or instrumental; it is also intrinsic to the good life—a life of honor, public esteem, and memorable reputation. Hence the other image Isocrates ends his oration with:

And how great must we think will be the name and the fame and the glory which they will enjoy during their lives, or, if they die in battle, will leave behind them—they who will have won the meed of honour in such an enterprise . . . what encomiums should we expect these men to win who have conquered the whole of Asia? For who that is skilled to sing or trained to speak will not labour and study in his desire to leave behind a memorial both of his own genius and of their valour, for all time to come? (186)

III

I have discussed the *Panegyricus* as an instance of wise deliberation, of phronesis, as Isocrates might have understood it and taught it to his students. And since phronein makes up only one constituent part of his rhetorical education, we must next turn to the other constituent part, legein, and examine how Isocrates might have linked the two together to produce the kind of public deliberation that would be compatible with his version of the art of rhetoric.

This may be a good place to note parenthetically that throughout Isocrates' writings, legein remains for modern readers a mystery. It is one of those commonsensical items of culture that needs no explanation, that everyone knows about, and that can be taken for granted. In a way *legein* seems to refer to the known procedures and practices of eloquence at the time. If this sounds too vague, it nevertheless conveys Isocrates' evasiveness, his reticence to talk about eloquence in any definite way other than in his frequently used and habitually indeterminate phrase *ta tou logou,* meaning "things" (commonplace knowledge or standard practices) "about eloquence." Still, this brief phrase is already an important indication of Isocrates' relation to the tradition of rhetoric: he does not understand himself as expanding the knowledge of the art as much as altering its uses and applications.[12] We will return to this discussion in the next chapter. The point to retain here is that the linking of phronein and legein cannot be expected to exhaust Isocrates' theory of eloquence but rather to address the question of the role he might have assigned to legein in its application to public deliberation.

If legein is truly integrated with phronein, then the role legein plays in deliberation is already made evident in Isocrates' remark about the *Panegyricus* as an oration that exemplifies the highest kind of oratory—to bring most benefit to those who hear while best displaying (*epideixis*) the ability of those who speak. The role of eloquence in the *Panegyricus,* therefore, can be none other than to display Isocrates' ability as rhetorician by performing the procedures he follows as he attempts to deliberate wisely on the good and the possible.

The symbolic enactment of deliberation already begins to take shape from the start, by the way Isocrates handles the question of hegemony at the beginning of the oration. The move to place the question of hegemony in the distant past and to address the issue at hand by undertaking a historical account betrays the caution and reservation associated with prudence. Even though the proposal has been made several times before, Isocrates will not go forward with the proposed course of action unless he positions the matter before him within the cultural past and examines it in the context of that culture and that history that have given Athens its identity and destiny. And it is this double context of cultural identity and historical destiny that the hymn of past Athens and the narrative of distant events in past Athens symbolically re-create. For what lies in the past are a handful of Athenians born of Attic soil and a core of human values that they cherished and by which they lived their lives. While the hymn of

Athens (of origins and lineage) undertakes the task of celebrating these values and their cultural transmission from generation to generation, the narrative of Athens (the development of agriculture, mystic rites, laws) undertakes the quite different task of recounting the events that led these first residents to consolidate themselves and to reach their destiny as free and self-governed agents of the polis.

Within this stable context of cultural identity and historical destiny, enacted symbolically through hymn and story, the question of an expedition can be revisited. Deliberation allows the present proposal to enter into a transaction with the past and the logic of the proposal to come in contact with the logic of a past identity and destiny. The course of action proposed finds a correlative in the past, and the logic of expansion finds its original analog. Now the hymn (of festivals and arts) celebrates not the core of Athenian values but their dissemination abroad, while the narrative (of the wars against the Trojans and the Amazons) turns its focus toward territorial expansion and conquest. Hymn and story coalesce to perform the meaning of power: a creation of human intelligence, the imposition of order on the world.[13]

But even when deliberation at present accords with traditional values and past events, the wise deliberating agent proceeds cautiously still, knowing that past precedent is no precept for the present. Advocacy is postponed once again, this time the proposal being placed in transaction with yet another narrative, the rise and fall of the Athenian Empire. And it is this last narrative that takes up the drive for power, acts out the double process that fuels the drive—reason and passion, the interest to obtain gain and security along with the passion of daring and fear—and performs the two radically different possible outcomes. First the two processes are placed in complementary positions to one another, the narrative events acquire a meaning of epic proportion, and the narrative turns to a heroic exaltation. Then the two are placed in antithetical relation to each other, the events narrated are invested with a meaning of tragic proportions, and the narrative gives way to lament.

Thus, even though the look to the past has not led to any solutions for the present, the artistic forms that this look assumed have delineated the nature of the problem by playing out on their formal texture the various potential scenarios that ensued and that could possibly ensue again. It remains up to the rest of the text, the advocacy portion of the *Panegyricus*, to take the necessary precaution and orchestrate the drive for power along complementary lines and to channel the thirst for expansion next to the need for security, the desire to dominate next to the fear of being enslaved, and the yearning for prosperity next to the apprehension for loss. And it is undoubtedly the mission of channeling a variety of drives in the same direction that the military and cultural analyses of the Persians are meant to serve.[14] The conclusion of these two analyses—the first, that "some of our possessions are now his, some will soon be his" (136), and the second, that "the barbarians are fit only to be used as household slaves" (181)—are quite compatible, and the reasoned response and passionate indignation they are meant to evoke are quite congruent. Hence the final certainty exhibited by Isocrates that the present advocacy will in fact unify all city-states, all factions in Athens, all calculations of interests and needs, all valued passions and desires. Hence also the final call to action: "we have it in our power to accomplish deeds as lofty as our dreams" (182).

The oration ends, then, by capturing artistically practical wisdom in deliberation and by performing symbolically the phronesis of the deliberating orator. Because phronesis comes with historical interpretation and cultural understanding, the orator's art must be applied to the task of telling stories and praising past people and events that foster insight and judgment in the audience as to their being and becoming, the wherefrom and the whereto of their existence. And while narratives and hymns must provide a historical and cultural context out of which deliberation emanates, they must also be used in a way that allows for change in the present and meets the particular demands on insight and judgment that the present situation makes. Once the dialectic between past and present is fixed, the orator displays phronesis by channeling all segments of society to the same end and by paying heed to link the action proposed with values revered and commitments cherished by all members of the polis.

Chapter Six

Educational Program

Isocrates' favorite way of defending his instruction against the fictional charge of corrupting the youth was to point to his past students. Quite clearly, he uses the form of apologia in the *Antidosis* as an alibi for a chance to recount his past accomplishments as an educator without being perceived as engaging in extravagant self-praise. Within the context of self-defense, his achievements, however numerous and detailed, emerge as appropriate responses to charges brought against him: "for [my accuser] declares that I have had as my pupils not only private persons but orators, generals, kings, and despots" (30). These responses include a list of men under his instruction "who were crowned by Athens with chaplets of gold" (94, 144), a lengthy passage of advice he gave to Timotheus (104ff.), an acknowledgment of presents he received from Nicocles (40), as well as numerous references to students he had taught and the fortunes he made from abroad (39, 147). Needless to say, these passages are invested with a good deal of the pride of an educator who was able to see student after student turn out well. More than that, they shift the focus of attention from teacher to student and change the terms of the discussion from the quality of instruction to the quality of its results. Throughout the *Antidosis* the success of students in private and public domains remains the sole criterion of the quality of instruction and the sole indicator of an educator's worth as a good and successful professional. If we are to believe Isocrates, this is not a criterion of his own choosing but one established by tradition and widely accepted by laymen and professional teachers alike: "for, I suppose, all men," he says, "are aware that a sophist reaps his finest and his largest reward when his pupils prove to be honourable and intelligent and highly esteemed by their fellow-citizens, since pupils of that sort inspire many with the desire to enjoy his teaching, while those who are depraved repel even those who were formerly minded to join his classes" (220). And so is the case also with professional educators, even the "teachers of philosophy," who, "however much they debate about the proper discipline of the soul . . . yet all are agreed on this, that the well-educated man must, as the result of his training in whatever discipline, show ability to deliberate and decide" (*To Nicocles* 51). Moreover, it is a criterion Isocrates willingly subjects himself to, asking directly his fictional detractor to consider whether "any of those who have been associated with me have turned out to be good men in their relations to the state, to their friends, and to their own households" (*Antidosis* 99).

I

The move to make students' practices the criterion of the quality of education is a crucial move. For it forecloses the possibility that educational training could be assessed solely on formal grounds or that instruction in a given matter could be evaluated entirely by standards provided by the field of study under question. The implicit challenge Isocrates issues to other educators, to produce evidence of results comparable to his own, should not be taken as an invitation to a contest in teaching achievements but as an indictment of a purely formalistic conception of education.[1] For when students' practices in the polis are kept in mind, it is truly difficult to think of education as a site sealed off from every other concern save the acquisition of knowledge, or to grasp learning as a process interested in no other transaction save the transmission of knowledge from teacher to student. By stressing the quality of private and public practices as a criterion of instruction, Isocrates limits the importance a student's access to knowledge has to the larger process of learning.

That the acquisition of knowledge comprises only a part of learning is most evident in a passage in which Isocrates puts forth his own view of the educational process. Students seeking to educate themselves in his or in any other field, he states,

must, first of all, have a natural aptitude for that which they have elected to do; secondly, they must submit to training and master the knowledge of their particular subject, whatever it may be in each case; and, finally, they must become versed and practiced in the use and application of their art; for only on these conditions can they become fully competent and pre-eminent in any line of endeavour. In this process, master and pupil each has his place; no one but the pupil can furnish the necessary capacity; no one but the master, the ability to impart knowledge; while both have a part in the exercises of practical application. (*Antidosis* 187–88)

Clearly, learning entails more than the task of acquiring knowledge ($\lambda\alpha\beta\epsilon\hat{\imath}\nu$ $\tau\grave{\eta}\nu\ \dot{\epsilon}\pi\iota\sigma\tau\acute{\eta}\mu\eta\nu$), a task which, in the terms of this passage, accounts for only one condition of learning: the process of training (paideusis). In addition to training, there are two other conditions: natural talent (physis) and practical application (empeiria), both of which link the acquisition of knowledge to the students' natural capacity to receive it and their learned ability to apply it. But as a more detailed look at the interrelationship among paideusis, physis, and empeiria suggests, this linking—contrary to what the passage above suggests—is one of subordination, not coordination. Paideusis is simply not on the same footing with either physis or empeiria.

The relative unimportance of instruction in things that must be known in a given field is made evident in sections 189–94 of *Antidosis*. He is quite explicit that, in the case of the art of oratory, natural talent and practical application are far more important than actual training in the knowledge pertaining to the field. A person blessed with natural talent has, he remarks, no real need of educational training, for "who does not know that such a man might, without the advantage of an elaborate education (*paideia*) and with only a superficial and common training, be an orator such as has never, perhaps, been seen among the Hellenes?" (*Antidosis* 190). Next in importance is empeiria which, though not as great a power as physis, can, in fact, have comparable results: "Again, we know that men who are less generously endowed by nature but excel in experience and practice (*empeiria kai epimeleia*), not only improve upon themselves, but surpass others who, though highly gifted, have been too negligent of their talents" (191). By contrast, no such preeminence in oratory could ever be attributed to the workings of paideia alone—something Isocrates is also explicit about: "These, then, are my views as to the relative importance of native ability (*physis*) and practice (*empeiria*). I cannot, however, make a like claim for education (*paideia*); its powers are neither equal nor comparable to theirs. For if one should take lessons in all the principles of oratory and master them with the greatest thoroughness, he might, perhaps, become a more pleasing speaker than most, but let him stand up before the crowd and lack one thing only, namely, assurance, and he would not be able to utter a word" (*Antidosis* 192). Without assurance, i.e., without an essential component of natural talent (191), instruction cannot accomplish very much. In contrast, both talent and experience can go very far without the aid of formal education. Everybody knows, he writes in *Against the Sophists*, that some men "who have never taken lessons from any one of the sophists have become able orators and statesmen" (14).

What lies beyond paideia is the kind of learning that results not from the acquisition of knowledge but from the uses to which knowledge is put. Again using the art of oratory as a case in point, Isocrates distinguishes knowledge from use:

I hold that to obtain a knowledge of the elements out of which we make and compose all discourses is not so very difficult.... But to choose from these elements those which should be employed for each subject, to join them together, to arrange them properly, and also, not to miss what the occasion demands ... these things, I hold, require much study (*epimeleia*) and are the task of a vigorous and imaginative mind: for this, the student must not only have the requisite aptitude but he must learn the different kinds of discourse (τὰ τῶν λόγων μαθεῖν) and practice himself in their use (περὶ δὲ τὰς χρήσεις αὐτῶν γυμνασθῆναι). (*Sophists* 16–17)

The two domains of learning, the acquisition of knowledge and the uses to which it may be put, are distinguished in terms of their relative degree of difficulty, the former being relatively easy to master, the latter requiring a great deal of diligence and zeal. More importantly, they are also distinguished in terms of the activity each performs. Acquisition of knowledge designates a cognitive activity that makes possible—without being a part of—another activity that pertains to the use and application of knowledge. Because knowledge itself cannot suggest the uses to which it can be put, it follows that instruction in a field of study will always be incomplete unless it cultivates the aptitude to know what to do with and how to use acquired knowledge. In the terms provided by the passage above, training in the field of oratory leads to a mastery of the elements of discourse; but such a mastery cannot help with the task of making choices, since it cannot answer such questions as how "to choose from these elements those which should be employed for each subject, to join them together, to arrange then properly, and also, not to miss what the occasion demands" (*Sophists* 16).

The two domains of learning distinguished in the passage above, then, also involve two distinct cognitive activities—something which is made clear only by the main clause of the second sentence: "these things, I hold, require much study and are the task of a vigorous and imaginative mind." What is translated here as "imaginative mind" appears in the original as *psyche doxastike*, a phrase that means literally a "conjecturing mind" and which must be understood in opposition to a knowing mind. A psyche doxastike is imaginative precisely because it does not fall within the purview of knowledge. Learning things about the field of oratory that can be known (λαβεῖν τὴν ἐπιστήμην), such as various types of discourses, is an easy task compared to that of learning matters based on opinion, such as combination of discourses, arrangement, and timeliness.[2] A mastery of the latter comes not with acquisition of knowledge but with practice and exercise in the use and application of knowledge or empeiria.

Finally, when Isocrates puts forth his own method of instruction, he turns the distinction between learning based on knowledge and learning based on the use and application of knowledge into a sequence, a progression from a lower to a higher level of study. Accordingly, teachers must initially "impart all the forms of discourse in which the mind expresses itself." After they have made their students "familiar and thoroughly conversant with these lessons," they must "set them at exercises, habituate them to work, and require them to combine in practice the particular things which they have learned, in order that they may grasp them more firmly and bring their theories into closer touch with the occasions for applying them—I say 'theories,' for no system of knowledge can possibly cover these occasions, since in all cases they elude our science" (*Antidosis* 184). The highest level of instruction pertains to "knowing" what particular things to apply to what occasion or, as the original suggests, how to bring one's opinion (doxa) closer to the contingent demands of the occasion (kairos): τῶν καιρῶν ἐγγυτέρω ταῖς δόξαις γένωνται.[3] The kind of learning Isocrates promotes, then, has to do with the ability to make experienced judgments in those affairs that present themselves full of uncertainty and ambiguity but which nevertheless must be addressed. For such affairs, always subject to situational contingencies, elude the province of knowledge (διαφεύγουσι τὰς ἐπιστήμας) and, inevitably, fall within the province of opinion.

II

As we have seen, the difference between Isocrates and other practicing educators does not revolve around instructional objectives concerning the mastery of a given field, but around educational ends regarding the uses such mastery might be put to in the real world. His disagreement with them is not a "disciplinary" one—in the modern sense of the term *discipline*.[4] He does not raise issues pertaining to specific fields, such as, for instance, what body of knowledge ought to constitute a given field, or how much of it a student ought to possess before that student could be said to have mastered that area of study. Isocrates challenges neither the legitimacy of specific fields of study nor the claims of practicing educators to be knowledgeable in them and to be able to impart their knowledge to students. His discourse does not bear the signals of an educator who demands his due recognition for having attained a specialized knowledge that is superior to theirs or for having improved the knowledge claims of an existing field of study more than they have. Rather, Isocrates questions the general premises of education and contests the dominant trends in educational activities of his times: the emphasis on acquisition of knowledge over its use, mastery of a field of study over its practical application, expertise over experience. His disagreement with other educators extends beyond the particulars of a given area of instruction, across disciplines, to general issues about learning—its pertinence to everyday practices, its value to human activity in the polis. The stance he assumes is that of an educator who keeps his eye on the larger picture, at once on the types of educational training available to the Athenians and on the significance that such training has to their lives and their polis.

Consistent with the broadness of this perspective, his critique of other educators seeks to appropriate, rather than displace, their instructional activities for broader educational ends. Far from posing himself as the alternative to the educational practices of his generation, Isocrates works with what already exists, invests normative instruction with new possibilities, and reorients standardized educational objectives toward novel ends. In turn, it is this impulse to appropriate rather than undermine existing educational practices that explains the frequent shifts in his attitude toward his opponents, this continuous wavering in the *Antidosis* from an all-out dismissal of educators to a qualified approbation or a reserved approval of their teaching. This impulse also explains why, when he puts forth his views about the type of educational training he considers most appropriate for Athenian youth, he includes the study of subjects he had been most critical about. As he envisions it in the *Antidosis,* the ideal curriculum would include, for example, the study of sciences, the very field he earlier condemned as irrelevant to "private or to public affairs" (262). For even though he considers instruction in astronomy and geometry to have no extrinsic value and no pertinence to students' "ability to speak and deliberate on affairs" (267), he recognizes the protreptic value of these studies and labels them "gymnastic of the mind" (266). Because such training would be more advanced and more helpful in disciplining and sharpening young minds (265) than the standardized, elementary instruction in grammar and music, he would place the study of astronomy and geometry at a level of instruction following the elementary level—a move that Beck has taken to signify "the growth of the idea of a secondary level of education" (262). According to Isocrates, a training in sciences would improve students' aptitude for mastering greater and more serious studies, or, at the very least, it would keep their minds occupied: "even if this learning can accomplish no other good, at any rate it keeps the young out of many other things which are harmful" (*Panathenaicus* 27).

Like the study of science, eristic philosophy is recognized by Isocrates as a field of study that can be valuable to the training of youth. He applauds the fact that eristic philosophers raise issues of "virtue and sobriety in their teaching" (*Sophists* 20) and finds their instruction to be a good preparation for philosophy, though not really entitled to the title of philosophy (*Antidosis* 266). He regards instruction in eristic philosophy to be appropriate for the education of youth at the secondary level of education (along with sciences) but not sufficient for the improvement of adults. With sciences as with eristic philosophy, then, Isocrates follows an identical procedure. In both cases his willingness to include these areas of study in the larger educational process is based on a distinction between a middle and a higher level of instruction, a training for youth and a training for adults, a training in all known fields of study and a training in the study of (his own version of) rhetoric and philosophy. If this distinction were to be granted, instruction in sciences and eristic philosophy would serve, as he says in reference to them, an important purpose: "I hold that for those who are at this age no more helpful or fitting occupation can be found than the pursuit of these studies; but for those who are older and for those who have been admitted to man's estate I assert that these disciplines are no longer suitable" (*Panathenaicus* 27–28). They are not suitable because the highest level of instruction is reserved exclusively for the study of rhetoric, the only area of study fitting to the education of adults. With rhetoric at the end of the educational process, the study of sciences and eristic philosophy acquires a preparatory function, providing students with ample occasions to sharpen their minds and develop their sense of discipline so that they may be best prepared to engage real learning when the time comes.

This rationale makes evident Isocrates' strategy of appropriation. Clearly, he mobilizes the protreptic value of other disciplines for his own educational objectives without challenging their legitimacy. Respecting their integrity as fields of study, he includes them in the educational process precisely as they are practiced in his day, proposing no internal changes, making no disciplinary revisions. But in imposing a hierarchy onto the educational process and in subordinating these studies to the study of rhetoric, he nullifies their claims to mastery and expertise—such that what was thus far understood as training leading to expertise is now regarded as training leading to a mere aptitude, a stage in learning that bears no other credentials than a readiness for subsequent learning. More importantly, the rearticulation of mastery and expertise as mere aptitudes for further study challenges prevailing notions that take educational training to be self-sufficient, and self-adequate, thereby exposing the purpose behind education as an issue that has yet to be resolved. For when mastery and expertise in a given area is no longer considered an end of instruction, then the end of instruction is up for discussion and, once again, open to debate.[5]

In the meantime, this strategy of appropriation, far from remaining at the level of abstraction, is put to practice in the *Antidosis*, vis-à-vis an area of study generally acknowledged to belong to the province of ancient philosophers: the making of genealogies. About this study, Isocrates' advice to youth is similar to the one he gave concerning the study of science and eristic philosophy, asking young men to "spend some time on these disciplines" but not "to allow their minds to be dried up by these barren subtleties, nor to be stranded on the speculations of the ancient sophists, who maintain, some of them, that the sum of things is made up of infinite elements; Empedocles that it is made up of four, with strife and love operating among them; Ion, of not more than three, Alcmaeon, of only two; Parmenides and Melissus, of one; and Gorgias, of none at all" (268). Though he claims that "such curiosities of thought are on a par with jugglers' tricks which, though they do not profit anyone, yet attract great crowds of the empty-minded" (269), he invokes their procedure and method of discussion when he expounds his own views of the art of rhetoric, prefacing his comments with this remark: "In my treatment of the art of discourse, I desire, like the genealogists, to start at the beginning" (180). In the ensuing discussion Isocrates utilizes ancient philosophers' manner of dealing with issues of origin and progress in their writings of genealogies or cosmologies. He moves from the make-up of human nature to traditional forms of instruction, draws a correspondence between the human body and instruction, establishes a hierarchy, and eventually ends by concluding that training in philosophy (his use of the term) is the most crucial human endeavor and the ultimate pursuit. In turn, this leads to an examination of the importance that such training has for human beings as well as to a discussion about the most appropriate method for that training. Predictably enough, all this turns out to be a justification of Isocrates' own subject and method of instruction. But the point here is not so much to determine whether Isocrates can match the vigor of pre-Socratic philosophers as it is to note the strategy of his procedure. For whether he has produced a sound genealogy of education or whether he has followed faithfully the motions of a cosmologist in his attempt to arrive at some final cause of things that explains all else, he does not stop there, does not pause to display the fruits of his inquiry, but goes on to argue for its pertinence and value to lived experience. As this example indicates, his method of appropriating other studies does not obtain by means of putting into effect some larger or more precise methodological apparatus but by putting what others have already done to a new use. His strategy is to open up accepted notions of expertise to a renegotiation.

In itself, then, mastery is not a problem Isocrates takes issue with. Neither in his critique of education nor in his appropriation of other studies does Isocrates challenge the claims of a given instruction to lead toward specialized knowledge or professional expertise. What he does contest is the premise that expertise may be the sole criterion of learning, that education ought to lead to a specialty or a technical profession: "these studies," he says in reference to sciences, "can be of no benefit to us after we have mastered them unless we have elected to make our living from this source" (264). He makes a similar point about the founders of forensic discourse, Corax and Tisias, whose rhetorical treatises reduced the art of rhetoric to the narrow specialty of forensic oratory and whose teachings gave the study of rhetoric over to the professional training of litigation experts (*Sophists* 19–20).

For Isocrates, expertise in a given subject is something requisite in all the arts but never enough in itself. His objection to educational activities of his day, as they are conducted in most arts, is that they put a premium on expertise without expending any effort on its application to culture— so much so that education has become the terrain which facilitates and oversees the production of uncultured experts:

> I observe that some of those who have become so thoroughly versed in these studies [geometry, astronomy, eristic disputations] as to instruct others in them fail to use opportunely the knowledge which they possess, while in other activities of life they are less cultivated than their students—I hesitate to say less cultivated than their servants. I have the same fault to find also with those who are skilled in oratory and those who are distinguished for their writings and in general with all who have superior attainments in the arts, in the sciences, and in specialized skill. (*Panathenaicus* 28–29)

With this sweeping remark, Isocrates condemns all training aspiring toward specialized knowledge, all learning leading to specialized practices and technical professions. Because current educators regard learning as a specialized activity that makes no allowances for cultivation in general culture, they produce professionals who cannot handle their own private affairs, specialists who cannot enter into civilized exchanges or graceful intercourse with their fellow citizens, experts who cannot participate in political decisions or even contribute to matters of public importance to all citizens.

Thus, the strategy of appropriating other fields of study and other educators does not always follow the logic of addition or improvement. His instruction in rhetoric and philosophy adds, as we have seen, onto the expertise prepared for and attained by means of instruction in other studies. But since his instruction is directed toward an arena of practices broadly defined as culture, which lies outside the grasp of academic expertise, the type of learning sought after by his educational program undermines the type of learning sought after by his competitors. Training in rhetoric presumes the acknowledgment of expertise as irrelevant to cultural practices, be they private, social, or political.

Let Isocrates' brief critique of Gorgias' private life (*Antidosis* 155–57), along with the more extended critique of dicastic orators, act here as a paradigmatic expression of successful teachers whose professional reputation cannot guard them from the disrepute they eventually fall into when they continue to disregard their private affairs. While failure to manage one's affairs has, in the case of a foreign professional such as Gorgias, no other consequence save the stigma attached to squandering one's wealth away, a similar failure in the case of a professional teacher who is also an Athenian citizen has far more serious consequences. Such a failure involves not just the person under question and that person's reputation but also the larger public whose resources must now be expended, directly or indirectly, to restore this unnecessary mishap. The choices left open to someone mismanaging private affairs are either to perform public duties and thereby receive benefits ordinarily reserved for the poor, or to spend one's days loitering around the courts, on the lookout for potential clients, encouraging litigation, and providing services to litigants, thereby making a living by preying on others. In the meantime, Isocrates' lengthy recounting of his own successful career as a professional teacher (*Antidosis* 144ff.) provides the opposite example, a case in point in which professionalism spills over into the domain of private affairs and the professional acts in a manner becoming not only to his profession but also to his standing as a private citizen. To be sure, Isocrates' personal narrative is a success story, the story of one who lost everything during the war but persevered, worked hard, and now has plenty to show for his efforts. But the highlights of that narrative—that he stayed away from the courts as well as from public offices and their compensations; that he received most of his income from foreign sources; and that he voluntarily enrolled himself as one of the twelve hundred richest Athenians, which brought onto him special levies—are not mere self-congratulatory gestures by a citizen who managed to turn himself into an asset for the polis; rather they are crucial markers of the various links that education can obtain between private and public life.

Let Isocrates' brief criticism of Timotheus (*Antidosis* 130–36), his beloved general and personal advisee, act here as a case in point that aptly demonstrates the tragedy of an uncultured expert, an unparalleled genius in the art of war and a violator of common decencies in social intercourse, a specialist in turning poorly funded expeditions into a profit for the state and a transgressor of the unwritten rule that a public figure must find the words to gain the public's favorable disposition.[6] Isocrates' criticism of Timotheus must have been rather difficult for him, for Timotheus not only represented the possible embodiment of Isocrates' political ideal, the only Athenian general able enough to actualize the Panhellenic dream, but he afforded Isocrates the only occasion the latter had to realize his professional ideal as a rhetorician: to occupy simultaneously the position of a teacher of rhetoric and the position of an adviser to the state.[7] To make matters even more difficult, he had sung Timotheus' praises earlier. But what appears in other writings as unreserved praise of Timotheus, and on one occasion even assumes the form of an encomium, in the *Antidosis* is interlaced with characteristics of a tragedy, and the laudatory discourse ends with Timotheus' emergence as a fallen figure whose otherwise perfect character is marked with the tragic flaw of pride: "because of his proud bearing—an advantage to the office of a general but out of place in dealing with men from day to day—everyone attributed to him the faults which I have named; for he was by nature as inept in courting the favour of men as he was gifted in handling affairs" (131). Acting as sound adviser, Isocrates had issued several warnings underscoring the fact that it is not enough for people in public offices to be of service to the state and to perform noble deeds: "they must at the same time not neglect to study and consider well how in everything they say and do they may convince the people of their graciousness and human sympathy; since those who are careless of these matters are thought by their fellow-citizens to be disagreeable and offensive" (*Antidosis* 132). In this manner, Isocrates assigns to goodwill (*eunoia*) an importance that surpasses the accomplishments of a general and to communication that secures goodwill a power that exceeds the authority of an expert.

Finally, let his frequent, brief references to teachers of political oratory act here as yet another indictment of expertise—the knowledge of a science about the future turn of events accompanied by a total incapacity "either of saying anything pertinent or of giving any counsel regarding the present" (*Sophists* 7), the learned experts who use their knowledge "not for the good of the state, but for what they themselves expect to gain" (*Panathenaicus* 12). Accomplished though they may be, such experts are, according to Isocrates, oblivious to the most elementary fact, "the fact that the government of the state is handed on by the older men to the youth of the coming generation; and that since the succession goes on without end, it follows of necessity that as is the education of our youth so from generation to generation will be the fortune of the state" (*Antidosis* 174). If this simple fact is taken into account, Isocrates believes, it will become evident that it is the affairs of the polis (τὰ κοινὰ τῆς πόλεως) "which should be the objects of our toil, of our study, and of our every act" (*Antidosis* 285). But then, this is what Isocrates' rhetorical education is all about: a training in oratory that will form students' political judgments.

III

Isocrates' antagonism toward contemporary educators was directed, then, against prevalent notions of education as expertise and of instruction as mastery of knowledge. Placing these notions within the context of lived practices at the individual, social, and political realms of existence, Isocrates supplemented existing views, demanding that knowledge be applied to lived experience and that expertise be made pertinent to everyday practices. The relation of his educational views to those of his contemporaries is best understood, then, in terms of a supplement, at once an addition and a change. Training in the application of knowledge is for Isocrates an advanced stage in the process of learning, an extension of a more basic stage that entails the mere acquisition of knowledge in a given subject matter. Understood in terms of a sequence and a progression, instruction in the application of knowledge emerges as a more advanced level of instruction, and Isocrates can be seen as charging preexisting methods of instruction with an added educational objective. Yet the process of applying knowledge to lived practices necessitates one's entrance into the domain of opinion, a domain wherein all cultural activity revolves.[8]

Having linked rhetorical education with political life, Isocrates gave to those aspiring to educate themselves a means for deliberating the destiny of their city. More than that, the link between rhetorical education and political life he sought to secure opened a space from within which it would be possible for Athenians to regard educational activities as so many occasions to make themselves proficient in political deliberation, public controversy, and societal debate. Naturally, it is fairly easy today to look down on a process of political deliberation that was not open to everyone, a public controversy that stopped short of social reforms, and a societal debate that left intact values upholding the policies of imperialism and slave ownership. But as I have been suggesting all along, the particular case of Isocrates' education challenges us to historicize our inquiry into human agency, acknowledge its situatedness, and recognize its provisionality. At the same time, it acts as an invaluable reminder to all of us of the political character of all education and the provisional character of all cultural politics.

Conclusion

Isocrates' rhetorical education put into practice Protagoras' vision of rhetoric as an art that could be infused with the demands of political life and could make students of rhetoric good citizens for the polis. Yet the turning of an outsider's vision into an Athenian reality proved to be infinitely more difficult than the mere implementation of a conception into practice. The Athens of Isocrates' time was qualitatively different from the Athens Protagoras had witnessed and had brought to his conception of rhetoric. With the success of the democratic experiment and with the fall of the Athenian empire, the gap between political equality and social inequality became more pronounced, and the polis ceased to be regarded as an integrated entity. To carry out Protagoras' educational project within the divided polis of the fourth century necessitated that the polis would be instituted once again as the common articulator of its citizens' collective interests. It was for that task that Isocrates turned to Gorgias' conception of rhetoric.

Isocrates borrowed Gorgias' notion of rhetoric as the power to create meaning and applied it to the public task of constituting the polis as an integrated community, an indissolubly single entity with tangible needs and identifiable desires. His writings created the sense of an unequivocal interdependence between citizenry and citizen and gave new life to the old maxim that what is good for the polis is good for the individual. Once the crafting power of discourse was given over to the task of creating and sustaining the illusion of a unified polis, rhetorical education could be reformulated as instruction in the process of discerning and advocating the common welfare, and rhetoric could be rearticulated as the art of deliberating publicly the good and possible for the polis. In Isocrates' reformulation and rearticulation of Protagoras' and Gorgias' versions of rhetoric, public speaking became tantamount to speaking for the polis and speaking for the polis became synonymous with the act of creating and sustaining the illusion of unity—an illusion given stability by narratives of communal values and shared commitments, credence by arguments about plausible solutions, and weight by the speaker's quality of character.

Isocrates' writings give us one of the final glimpses in the history of rhetoric of community as a unified collectivity, and perhaps the last successful deployment of rhetoric against the forces of fragmentation and the pressures of difference. It is a dream that can no longer be dreamed in the present era of nation-states, and an ideal that can no longer be attached to rhetoric. Nevertheless, the dream can still be activated in the local scene. Local efforts toward unification and concerted action can learn a great deal from Isocratean rhetoric, for the act of speaking for the polis, as Isocrates put it forth, may very well outlive the historical purpose it was given and, in the absence of the polis, may very well find new life in contemporary local struggles. In our own times speaking for the polis may still designate a way of speaking in the world that articulates speakers and audiences as social beings and discourse as the ground for binding individuals together into a potential community. In this way of speaking the struggles for concerted action reach out to the history of the community whose discursively crafted narratives illuminate the cultural limits and possibilities of the community's horizon of political and ethical becoming.

Notes

Introduction

1. Jebb, 2: 1–260.

2. Freeman, 179–209; Jaeger, 3: 46–155; Beck, 253–300; Marrou, 79–91; Kennedy, 70–74, 174–203.

3. See, for example, Harold Barrett, *The Sophists*; Brian Vickers, "Territorial Disputes," in *In Defence of Rhetoric*, 148–213.

4. *Sophistical Rhetoric in Classical Greece.*

5. See, for example, Susan Jarratt, *Rereading the Sophists*; Roger Moss, "The Case for Sophistry."

6. Kathleen Welch, "Writing Instruction in Ancient Athens"; Samuel Ijsseling, *Rhetoric and Philosophy in Conflict*, pp. 1–33.

7. See McGee, "The Moral Problem of *Argumentum* per *Argumentum*."

8. See "Epideictic Rhetoric as Social Hegemony"; "Toward a Cultural Understanding of Classical Epideictic Oratory."

9. See my "Human Agency in the History of Rhetoric."

10. For the nature of the educational debate and the various factions involved, see Marrou 85–87; Kennedy 177–90; and Jaeger 3: 67–70. For contemporary relevance of that debate, see Kathleen Welch, *The Contemporary Reception of Classical Rhetoric*, 3–33.

11. For the differences in ethical, social, and political perspectives on education, see Jaeger 3: 132–55.

12. On the forging of the "we" in sociopolitical movements, see Laclau and Mouffe, *Hegemony and Socialist Strategy*; Hall, *The Hard Road to Renewal*.

Chapter One: Rhetoric and Social Cohesion

1. On ancient commentary about the treatise, see Kennedy, *The Art of Persuasion in Greece*, 70ff.; for a perspective on Isocrates' theory of rhetoric, based on the absence of that treatise, see also Michael Cahn, "Reading Rhetoric Rhetorically: Isocrates and the Marketing of Insight."

2. Thucydides treats them with scorn, Aristophanes with ridicule, *Wealth* 898–919.

3. According to Aristophanes, there was an entire class of people (something like today's brokers) who made a living by bringing together sophists and wealthy clients.

4. See W. K. C. Guthrie's discussion, pp. 63–68.

5. See Juha Sihvola, *Decay, Progress, the Good Life?*

6. See passage on 352ff., but also context of the discussion, 332–71.

7. On the ontological significance of using language to shape the real, see Hans Blumenberg, "An Anthropological Approach to the Contemporary Significance of Rhetoric."

8. *Suppliants* 201–4.

9. Sihvola 95–103. See also E. R. Dodds, *The Ancient Concept of Progress.*

10. Blumenberg, "Sophists and Cynics," p. 334.

11. For another meaning of Isocrates' use of the term *hegemon,* see Ijsseling's chapter on Isocrates. For the importance of the term in Isocrates' rhetorical theory, see John Poulakos, "Early Changes in Rhetorical Practice and Understanding."

12. On the oratorical practices in the assembly, see Joint Association, *The World of Athens: An Introduction to Classical Athenian Culture,* pp. 199–206; A. H. M. Jones, *Athenian Democracy* 42–50. See also M. I. Finley, "Ancient Demagogues"; H. Hudson-Williams, "Political Speeches in Athens"; Stanley Wilcox, "Isocrates' Fellow-Rhetoricians."

13. Even though the link expressed here between rhetoric and the audience's self-understanding carries poststructuralist overtones, note its pertinence to the appeal made by Isocrates in the last paragraph of the *Panegyricus.* For a general background on contemporary views of rhetoric, see Kenneth Burke, *Language as Symbolic Action;* Thomas Farrell, *Norms of Rhetorical Culture;* Walter Fisher, *Human Communication as Narration;* Jurgen Habermas, *Legitimation Crisis;* Gerard Hauser, *Introduction to Rhetorical Theory;* Michael Leff, "In Search of Ariadne's Thread"; Richard McKeon, "Uses of Rhetoric in a Technological Age"; Raymie McKerrow, "Critical Rhetoric"; James Murphy, *A Synoptic History of Classical Rhetoric;* Paul Ricoeur, *The Rule of Metaphor;* Brian Vickers, *In Defence of Rhetoric.*

14. The compatibility between self-understanding and action was also noted by Plato, who divided audiences in the *Phaedrus* according to different types of souls.

15. On the property of language to resolve real irresolutions, see Lloyd F. Bitzer, "The Rhetorical Situation"; see also Fredric Jameson's first chapter of *The Political Unconscious.*

16. On the relationship between speech and political agency in classical democracy, see Jean-Pierre Vernant, *The Origins of Greek Thought,* pp. 49–68.

17. See Guthrie's discussion of Thrasymachus, pp. 294–98; see also Sprague 86–93.

18. For a comprehensive study of Gorgias' theory of persuasion, see Charles Segal, "Gorgias and the Psychology of the Logos."

19. See John Poulakos' chapter on Plato's reception of the Sophists, 74.

20. Something already suggested by Protagoras' view of language. See Sihvola 108–12.

21. Throughout the *Antidosis* Isocrates explicitly ties his instruction to public and private interests, *idion kai koinon.*

22. On the changing attitudes of intellectuals following Protagoras, see Cynthia Farrar, *The Origins of Democratic Thinking*, pp. 99ff.

23. See G. B. Kerferd's chapter on sophistic relativism in *The Sophistic Movement* (83–110).

24. For the relation of logos to the nomos-physis controversy, see Guthrie 55–134; Kerferd, *The Sophistic Movement*, pp. 111–30.

25. Segal makes the argument that the manipulative operations of logos in Gorgias' *Helen* include the listener's voluntary participation (107–12).

Chapter Two: Speaking Like a Citizen

1. On the relationship between these orations, see Jaeger 3: 84–105.

2. On the historical background and Isocrates' relation to tyrants, see Jaeger 3: 87ff.; Norman Baynes, "Isocrates."

3. On Isocrates' use of his works as textbooks, see Kennedy, *The Art of Persuasion in Greece*, pp. 178ff.; Marrou 84–85; R. Johnson, "Isocrates' Methods of Teaching."

4. On the specifics of Isocrates' school, see Marrou 80–84; Beck 258–61.

5. On the link between Protagoras' rhetorical education and civic virtue, see Farrar 44–98; on Protagoras' civic ideals as reflection of existing democratic ideals, see Schiappa 168–71.

6. An exception is the attitude he expresses in the *Areopagiticus*, pp. 43–49; but this concerns the youth.

7. Citizenly conduct, for Isocrates, concerns mainly adults.

8. On this, see Daniel Gillis, "The Ethical Basis of Isocratean Rhetoric."

9. For the interrelationship between the moral and the political, see Philip Neserius, "Isocrates' Political and Social Ideas."

10. On the impact of orators on collective decisions, see Josiah Ober, *Mass and Elite in Democratic Athens*, 127–37, 166–70.

11. Ober 141–48.

12. See W. R. Connor, *The New Politicians of Fifth-Century Athens*.

13. Food and health metaphors are used to characterize rhetoric throughout the *Gorgias*.

14. Not all public officers took advantage of the democratic administrative machinery. See Jones 99–133.

15. On the parasitical potential of rhetoric, see Jacques Derrida, "Plato's Pharmacy."

16. Hence his characterization of the good orator as *kyrios*, someone in charge of the household.

17. Ober 205ff.

18. As in the *Phaedrus*, where Socrates' discussion of the dialectic process comes as a critique of Lysias' craft with speech-making. For a favorable reading of Lysias' speech, see Nussbaum 207–10.

19. Gorgias' defense of the art of rhetoric in the *Gorgias* is repeatedly made by connecting rhetoric to other arts and by distinguishing an art itself from its potentially good or evil uses.

20. On mercenary armies and their deployment in Greek warfare at that time, see John Fine, *The Ancient Greeks*, pp. 532–34.

21. For a portrait of Alcibiades, see Will Durant, *The Life of Greece*, pp. 443–45.

22. For logos as instigator of tarache in the listener's psyche, see Charles Segal, "Gorgias and the Psychology of the Logos."

23. This is compatible with Gorgias' theory of persuasion in the *Encomium of Helen.*

Chapter Three: Human Agency

1. On political divisions, see M. I. Finley, *Politics in the Ancient World*, pp. 50–69, 97–121; W. R. Connor, *The New Politicians of Fifth-Century Athens*, esp. pp. 5–9; David Stockton, *The Classical Athenian Democracy*, pp. 117–40. For a general background in politics and Isocrates' relation to politics, see James Davidson, "Isocrates Against Imperialism"; Eric Havelock, *The Liberal Temper in Greek Politics*; M. L. W. Laistner, "The Influence of Isocrates' Political Doctrines"; Robert Moysey, "Isocrates and Chares"; S. Perlman, "Panhellenism, the Polis and Imperialism"; Wesley Thompson, "Isocrates on the Peace Treaties"; Frank Vatai, *Intellectuals in Politics in the Greek World.* On social divisions, see Jones 75–98; Halperin 88–112; Page Dubois, *Sowing the Body.* On economic divisions, see Ste Croix 31–204; Wood 81–125. On the disparity between political equality and socio-economic inequality, see Wood 126–36. For a general background in ancient economy, see Perry Anderson, *Passages from Antiquity to Feudalism*; M. T. W. Arnheim, *Aristocracy in Greek Society*; M. M. Austin and P. Vidal-Naquet, *Economic and Social History of Ancient Greece*; John Davies, *Athenian Propertied Families* and *Wealth and the Power of Wealth in Classical Athens*; M. I. Finley, *Economy and Society in Ancient Greece*; Alexander Fuks, "Isocrates and the Social-Economic Situation in Greece."

2. Ober 293–314.

3. Farrar 28–38.

4. The socio-economic inequality is often unaccounted for by arguments upholding Protagoras' ideals as a reflection of Athenian ideals; see Schiappa 175–80.

5. Schiappa 77–81.

6. The "man measure" fragment finds its way to the core in ethical discussions on the tension between relativity and ethical standards; see Guthrie 164–76; Kerferd, *The Sophistic Movement*, pp. 83–110.

7. Farrar 28–38.

8. See her two chapters on Protagoras.

9. John Poulakos, *Sophistical Rhetoric in Classical Greece*, pp. 64–67.

10. This is supported by Protagoras' argument immediately following the "Great Speech" in the *Protagoras*, about the hypothetical city of flute players.

11. On the conduct of the Athenian empire toward the allied city-states, see Fine 329–82.

12. See Guthrie 101–17.

13. For a background on Gorgias, see Sprague 30–67; on Gorgias' fragments,

see Hermann Diels and Walter Kranz, *Die Fragmente der Vorsokratiker*. See also Sharon Crowley, "Of Gorgias and Grammatology." For a general background on the Sophists, see Jacqueline de Romilly, *The Great Sophists in Periclean Athens;* Eugène Dupreel, *Les Sophistes;* G. B. Kerferd, *The Sophists and Their Legacy;* Jane Sutton, "Rereading Sophistical Arguments."

14. Farrar 106–09.

15. Farrar 106–09.

16. An understanding created primarily by Plato's *Gorgias.*

17. On the process of persuasion and the power Gorgias assigns to logos, see John Poulakos, "Gorgias' *Encomium to Helen* and the Defense of Rhetoric."

18. A point argued convincingly by Segal.

19. See Jacqueline de Romilly, "Gorgias et le pouvoir de la poésie."

20. See Bruce Gronbeck, "Gorgias on Rhetoric and Poetic."

21. On the irreconcilable demands made on reason during the tragic situation, see Hans Blumenberg, "An Anthropological Approach," pp. 447–56.

22. Blumenberg, "An Anthropological Approach," pp. 447ff.

23. See Martha Nussbaum's discussion on the motivational function of desire, *Fragility of Goodness*, pp. 214–15.

24. See Jacqueline de Romilly's chapter on "Gorgias and Magic" in her *Magic and Rhetoric in Ancient Greece.*

25. See Nussbaum's argument on pp. 200–233, which frames her reading of the *Phaedrus*—that, eventually, Plato changed his mind about desire.

26. On the differences between the Athenian empire and Isocrates' vision of Athens as a leader of a city-state coalition, see my reading of the *Panegyricus* in "Recovering the Voices of the Text."

27. See Norlin's concluding remarks in his general introduction to Isocrates.

28. Isocrates' notion of honorable reputation is starkly different from Plato's more general notion of fame.

29. See de Romilly, "Eunoia in Isocrates or the Political Importance of Creating Good Will."

30. See Michael McGee's discussion of Isocrates' notion of character in "The Moral Problem of *Argumentum* per *Argumentum*."

31. See Richard Weaver, "The *Phaedrus* and the Nature of Rhetoric."

32. See Nussbaum's discussion of love and madness in her chapter on the *Symposium* and her chapter on the *Phaedrus*.

33. Michel Foucault, *The Use of Pleasure,* pp. 229–46.

34. So is, for Isocrates, the proper way of accumulating wealth.

35. In this he is comparing professional orators to professional generals; see the remarks on Timotheus in the *Antidosis* (101ff.) and the praise that a good general knows how to use the means with which the state avails him wisely and turn them to profit (seize other ships, etc.).

36. *The Use of Pleasure* 229–46.

37. He makes the same remark several times in praising Evagoras.

38. See "Isocrates on Rhetoric and Power."

Chapter Four: Eloquence and Reflection

1. *Paideia* 3: 90.

2. On rhetoric's connections to the courts and the assembly, see Ober 104–55. On the development of rhetoric in the classical period, see Thomas Cole, *The Origins of Rhetoric in Ancient Greece*; Richard Leo Enos, *Greek Rhetoric Before Aristotle*.

3. On legal transformations, see Douglass MacDowell, *The Law in Classical Athens*; Richard Garner, *Law and Society in Classical Athens*. On legislative transformations, see David Stockton, *The Classical Athenian Democracy*; A. H. M. Jones, *Athenian Democracy*. For a general historical background, see Robert J. Bonner, *Lawyers and Litigants in Ancient Athens*; M. I. Finley, *Ancient History*; George Grote, *A History of Greece*; Jean-Pierre Vernant, *Myth and Thought Among the Greeks*.

4. Stockton 19–56.

5. Stockton 84–95.

6. For the shift from secret to open practices, and from a private to an open society, see Vernant, *The Origins of Greek Thought*, pp. 38–68.

7. Ober 182–91.

8. Garner 58–94.

9. MacDowell 58–62.

10. MacDowell 58–62.

11. On the practices of logography and their evolutions, see Richard Enos, *Greek Rhetoric Before Aristotle*, pp. 23–40.

12. *Antidosis* 40. On Isocrates' teaching and influence, see Charles Adams, "Recent Views of the Political Influence of Isocrates"; Goodwin Berquist, "Isocrates of Athens"; Diogenes Laertius, *Lives*; Dionysius of Halicarnassus, *The Critical Essays*; M. I. Finley, "The Heritage of Isocrates," in his *Use and Abuse of History*; R. Johnson, "A Note on the Number of Isocrates' Pupils"; Stanley Wilcox, "The Scope of Early Rhetorical Instruction."

13. Isocrates never mentions in his writings that he had been a logographer, even though there are several extant writings by him suggesting otherwise.

14. He presents this instructional combination as having created envy in other teachers of oratory; *Antidosis* 243. On Isocrates' theory of rhetoric, see William Benoit, "Isocrates and Aristotle on Rhetoric" and "Isocrates and Plato on Rhetoric and Rhetorical Education"; G. J. De Vries, "Isocrates' Reaction to the *Phaedrus*"; Monique Dixsaut, "Isocrate contre des sophistes sans sophistique"; Robert Gaines, "Isocrates, EP. 6.8"; W. R. Johnson, "Isocrates Flowering"; George Kennedy, "Isocrates' *Encomium of Helen*"; John Poulakos, "Gorgias' and Isocrates' Use of the Encomium"; Jean-François de Raymond, "Isocrates et le langage de la culture"; Erika Rummel, "Isocrates' Ideal of Rhetoric"; Russell Wagner, "The Rhetorical Theory of Isocrates."

15. On the term *rhetoric* and its association with politics, see W. R. Connor's discussion on the new vocabulary of politics and new terms for leaders, pp. 99–118. On Isocrates' relation to philosophy and Plato, see R. L. Howland, "The Attack on Isocrates in the *Phaedrus*"; Terry Perkins, "Isocrates and Plato"; Wayne Sheeks,

"Isocrates, Plato, and Xenophon against the Sophists"; Stanley Wilcox, "Criticisms of Isocrates and His *philosophia.*"

16. On the important role of improvisation in rhetorical training, see Tony Lentz, *Orality and Literacy in Hellenic Greece;* on Isocrates' departure from the tradition, see the discussion on pp. 122–35.

17. Isocrates can, in fact, be considered a pioneer cultural critic, for the issues he addressed were always much broader than the political issues addressed by the assembly.

18. I am using these terms to suggest not the inclusivity they typically connote but a terrain larger than the practices of policy-making of the assembly, a more general sphere inclusive of general issues as proposed in festivals and discussed in the agora.

19. On the shift in Isocrates from orality to writing, see Lentz 122–35.

20. For the capacity of rhetoric to retard action, see Hans Blumenberg, "An Anthropological Approach to the Contemporary Significance of Rhetoric."

21. See note 18 above.

22. On Isocrates' relation to poetry, see Helen North, "The Use of Poetry in the Training of the Ancient Orator." On oratorical uses of poetic seduction, see Thomas Rosenmeyer, "Gorgias, Aeschylus, and *Apate.*" On Isocrates' relation to the tradition of epideictic rhetoric and encomiastic praise, see Theodore C. Burgess, "Epideictic Literature"; Nicole Loraux, *The Invention of Athens;* Christine Oravec, "'Observation' in Aristotle's Theory of Epideictic"; William Race, "Pindaric Encomium and Isokrates' *Evagoras*"; Lawrence Rosenfield, "The Practical Celebration of Epideictic"; Brian Vickers, "Epideictic and Epic in the Renaissance."

23. On Isocrates' art, see Andrew Ford, "The Price of Art in Isocrates."

24. "Isocrates' Use of Narrative in the *Evagoras.*"

Chapter Five: Public Deliberation

1. Norlin's comment on the occasion of the *Panegyricus* wavers: "The title was chosen by Isocrates himself, no doubt to signify its appropriateness to be delivered before a pan-Hellenic gathering at Olympia, where Gorgias and Lysias had actually spoken on the same theme before him. It is, however, certain that it was not delivered by Isocrates; and, although it may have been read aloud on such an occasion by another, it was probably written as a political pamphlet and circulated among a reading public" (1: 119).

2. Near the end of *Panathenaicus* (200ff.), Isocrates mentions in great detail an event of revising one of his works with the help of three of his students; of summoning a former student to come and help them; of having lengthy arguments with that student; of having some public gathering formed around the two of them; and, finally, of engaging and being engaged by a couple of people gathered. This scene gives us valuable information as to how Isocrates' works are written and also as to how they were disseminated to a public that was not necessarily a reading public. On literacy in Classical Greece, see Eric Havelock, *The Literate Revolution in Greece.*

3. As some of the passages quoted make evident, Isocrates still uses *sophia* to mean practical wisdom.

4. On the importance of luck to ethics, see Martha Nussbaum, whose book *Fragility of Goodness* is subtitled *Luck and Ethics in Greek Tragedy and Philosophy.*

5. On Isocrates' use of the past, see my "Isocrates' Use of Narrative in the *Evagoras.*" On his relation to history, see Charles Hamilton, "Greek Rhetoric and History"; Robert Wallace, "The Date of Isokrates' *Areopagiticus*"; Bradford C. Welles, "Isocrates' View of History." On the general relationship between rhetoric and history, see James Berlin, "Revisionary History"; John Angus Campbell, "A Rhetorical Interpretation of History"; Paul Ricoeur, *Hermeneutics and the Human Sciences.*

6. See S. Perlman, "Panhellenism, the Polis and Imperialism."

7. Isocrates has not guarded against the interpretation that his call for panhellenism may in fact be a pretense for another instance of Athenian imperialism; see Frank Vatai's reading of the *Panegyricus* in the context of panhellenism and imperialism in his *Intellectuals in Politics in the Greek World,* pp. 99–111. On Isocrates' relation to imperialistic politics, see Minor Markle, "Support of Athenian Intellectuals for Philip"; Philip Merlan, "Isocrates, Aristotle and Alexander the Great"; Robert Moysey, "Isokrates' *On the Peace*"; S. Perlman, "Isocrates' 'Philippus'—A Reinterpretation."

8. On autonomy and freedom, see Guthrie 148–63.

9. As far as I can tell, historians and tragedians before Isocrates use the term *patris* in a strict sense, meaning the actual place of one's origins (place always being understood as a polis, not a nation).

10. See S. Perlman, "Panhellenism, the Polis and Imperialism."

11. Nussbaum makes a similar point in her discussion of the role of tyche in Aristotle; see her *Fragility of Goodness,* pp. 290–317.

12. Except in his earlier works, in which he saw himself contributing to the genre of the encomium; see the opening remarks he makes in two encomia, *Helen* and *Busiris;* in both he criticizes selections of topoi made by earlier orators in their encomiastic praises.

13. This coincides with Thucydides' notion of power; see Farrar's chapter on Thucydides, pp. 126–91.

14. For earlier uses of the Persians as an appeal for Greek consolidation, see François Hartog, *The Mirror of Herodotus.*

Chapter Six: Educational Program

1. See my "Isocratean Rhetorical Education."

2. The following passage in reference to the composition of the *Antidosis* suggests that for Isocrates the most difficult aspect of composition was the unification of various discourses under a common theme: "Now to view as a whole so great an extent of subject matter, to harmonize and bring together so many diverse varieties of discourse, to connect smoothly what follows with what goes before, and to make all parts consonant one with another, was by no means an easy undertaking" (*Antidosis* 11).

3. On Isocrates' notion of kairos, see Michael Cahn, "Reading Rhetoric Rhetorically."

4. On Isocrates' content-specific approach to education, see Beck 272–82; see also James Jarrett, *The Educational Theories of the Sophists*.

5. Isocrates extends educational debates beyond his educational treatises and makes them part of his orations. See, for instance, opening discussion in the *Helen*.

6. See Jacqueline de Romilly, "Eunoia in Isocrates."

7. For Isocrates' notion of leadership and the role of himself as an adviser to the leader, see Jaeger 3: 84–105. To Jaeger's excellent position, an added observation needs to be made: namely, that Isocrates saw himself as adviser to the leader following his failure to advise the democratic polis, for the *Panegyricus* shows plainly that Isocrates regarded himself as an adviser to the people.

8. On views about intellectuals in ancient Athens, see Blair Campbell, "Thought and Political Action in Athenian Tradition"; K. J. Dover, "The Freedom of the Intellectual in Greek Society." On current views of intellectuals, see Henry Giroux et al., "The Need for Cultural Studies."

Works Cited

Adams, Charles. "Recent Views of the Political Influence of Isocrates." *Classical Philology* 7 (1912): 343–50.

Aeschylus. *Prometheus Bound.* Trans. H. W. Smyth. London: William Heinemann, 1927.

Anderson, Perry. *Passages from Antiquity to Feudalism.* London: New Left Books, 1974.

Aristophanes. *The Clouds.* Trans. B. B. Rogers. London: William Heinemann, 1926.

———. *Wealth.* Trans. B. B. Rogers. London: William Heinemann, 1927.

Aristotle. *The Art of Rhetoric.* Trans. J. H. Freese. London: William Heinemann, 1982.

———. *Athenian Constitution, Eudemian Ethics.* Trans. H. Rackham. London: William Heinemann, 1981.

———. *Politics.* Trans. H. Rackham. London: William Heinemann, 1977.

———. *Rhetorica Ad Alexandrum.* Trans. W. S. Hett and H. Rackham. London: William Heinemann, 1983.

Arnheim, M. T. W. *Aristocracy in Greek Society.* London: Thames and Hudson, 1977.

Austin M. M., and P. Vidal-Naquet. *Economic and Social History of Ancient Greece.* Berkeley: University of California Press, 1977.

Barrett, Harold. *The Sophists: Rhetoric, Democracy, and Plato's Idea of Sophistry.* Novato, Calif.: Chandler and Sharp, 1987.

Baynes, Norman. "Isocrates." In his *Byzantine Studies and Other Essays,* 144–67. London: Athlone, 1955.

Beck, Frederick. *Greek Education 450–350 BC.* New York: Barnes and Noble, 1964.

Benoit, William. "Isocrates and Aristotle on Rhetoric." *Rhetoric Society Quarterly* 20 (1990): 251–60.

———. "Isocrates and Plato on Rhetoric and Rhetorical Education." *Rhetoric Society Quarterly* 21 (1991): 60–72.

Berlin, James. "Revisionary History: The Dialectical Method." *Pre/Text* 8 (1987): 47–61.

Berquist, Goodwin. "Isocrates of Athens: Foremost Speech Teacher of the Ancient World." *Speech Teacher* 8 (1959): 251–55.

Bitzer, Lloyd F. "The Rhetorical Situation." *Philosophy and Rhetoric* 1 (1968): 1–14.

Blass, Frederick. *Isocratis Orationes.* Leipzig: Teubner, 1889.

Blumenberg, Hans. "An Anthropological Approach to the Contemporary Significance of Rhetoric." In *After Philosophy: End or Transformation?*, edited by Kenneth Baynes, James Bohman, and Thomas McCarthy, 429–58. Cambridge: MIT Press, 1987.

———. "Sophists and Cynics: Antithetical Aspects of the Prometheus Material." In *Work on Myth*, translated by Robert Wallace, 328–49. Cambridge: MIT Press, 1985.

Bonner, Robert J. *Lawyers and Litigants in Ancient Athens.* Chicago: University of Chicago Press, 1927.

Burgess, Theodore C. "Epideictic Literature." In his volume 3 of *Studies in Classical Philology,* 89–261. Chicago: University of Chicago Press, 1902.

Burke, Kenneth. *Language as Symbolic Action.* Berkeley: University of California Press, 1966.

———. *The Philosophy of Literary Form.* Berkeley: University of California Press, 1973.

Cahn, Michael. "Reading Rhetoric Rhetorically: Isocrates and the Marketing of Insight." *Rhetorica* 7 (1989): 121–44.

Campbell, Blair. "Thought and Political Action in Athenian Tradition: The Emergence of the 'Alienated' Intellectual." *History of Political Thought* 5 (1984): 17–59.

Campbell, John Angus. "A Rhetorical Interpretation of History." *Rhetorica* 2 (1984): 227–66.

Classen, C. Joachim. "Aristotle's Picture of the Sophists." In *The Sophists and Their Legacy,* edited by G. B. Kerferd, 7–24. Wiesbaden: Franz Steiner, 1981.

Cole, Thomas. *The Origins of Rhetoric in Ancient Greece.* Baltimore: Johns Hopkins University Press, 1991.

Connor, W. R. *The New Politicians of Fifth-Century Athens.* Princeton: Princeton University Press, 1971.

Crowley, Sharon. "Of Gorgias and Grammatology." *College Composition and Communication* 30 (1979): 279–84.

Davidson, James. "Isocrates Against Imperialism: An Analysis of the *De Pace.*" *Historia* 39 (1990): 20–36.

Davies, John. *Athenian Propertied Families.* Oxford: Oxford University Press, 1971.

———. *Wealth and the Power of Wealth in Classical Athens.* Salem, N.H.: Ayer, 1981.

de Romilly, Jacqueline. "Eunoia in Isocrates or the Political Importance of Creating Good Will." *Journal of Hellenic Studies* 78 (1958): 92–101.

———. "Gorgias et le pouvoir de la poésie." *Journal of Hellenic Studies* 93 (1973): 155–62.

———. *The Great Sophists in Periclean Athens.* Trans. Janet Lloyd. Oxford: Clarendon Press, 1992.

———. *Magic and Rhetoric in Ancient Greece.* Cambridge: Harvard University Press, 1975.

Derrida, Jacques. "Plato's Pharmacy." In *Dissemination,* translated by Barbara Johnson, 63–171. Chicago: University of Chicago Press, 1981.

De Vries, G. J. "Isocrates' Reaction to the *Phaedrus.*" *Mnemosyne* 6 (1953): 39–45.

Diels, Hermann, and Walther Kranz, eds. *Die Fragmente der Vorsokratiker.* 3 vols. Berlin: Weidmann, 1952.

Diogenes Laertius. *Lives.* Trans. R. D. Hicks. London: William Heinemann, 1925.

Dionysius of Halicarnassus. *The Critical Essays.* Trans. S. Usher. Cambridge: Cambridge University Press, 1974.

Dixsaut, Monique. "Isocrate contre des sophistes sans sophistique." In *Le Plaisir de parler: Études de sophistique comparée,* edited by Barbara Cassin. Paris: Les Éditions de Minuit, 1986.

Dodds, E. R. *The Ancient Concept of Progress.* Oxford: Clarendon Press, 1973.

Dover, K. J. "The Freedom of the Intellectual in Greek Society." *Talanta* 7 (1976): 24–54.

Dubois, Page. *Sowing the Body: Psychoanalysis and Ancient Representations of Women.* Chicago: University of Chicago Press, 1988.

Dupreel, Eugène. *Les Sophistes.* Neuchatel: Editions du Griffon, 1948.

Durant, Will. *The Life of Greece.* New York: Simon and Schuster, 1939.

Enos, Richard Leo. "The Epistemology of Gorgias' Rhetoric: A Re-Examination." *Southern Speech Communication Journal* 42 (1976): 35–51.

———. *Greek Rhetoric Before Aristotle.* Prospect Heights, Ill.: Waveland Press, 1993.

Euripides. *Suppliants.* London: William Heinemann, 1912.

Farrar, Cynthia. *The Origins of Democratic Thinking: The Invention of Politics in Classical Athens.* Cambridge: Cambridge University Press, 1988.

Farrell, Thomas. *Norms of Rhetorical Culture.* New Haven: Yale University Press, 1993.

Fine, John. *The Ancient Greeks: A Critical History.* Cambridge: Harvard University Press, 1983.

Finley, M. I. *Ancient History.* New York: Penguin, 1987.

———. "Athenian Demagogues." *Past and Present* 21 (1962): 3–24.

———. *Economy and Society in Ancient Greece.* New York: Viking, 1981.

———. "The Heritage of Isocrates." In his *The Use and Abuse of History,* 193–214. New York: Penguin, 1975.

———. *Politics in the Ancient World.* Cambridge: Cambridge University Press, 1983.

Fisher, Walter. *Human Communication as Narration: Toward a Philosophy of Reason, Value, and Action.* Columbia: University of South Carolina Press, 1987.

Ford, Andrew. "The Price of Art in Isocrates: Formalism and the Escape from Politics." In *Rethinking the History of Rhetoric,* edited by Takis Poulakos, 31–52. Boulder: Westview Press, 1993.

Foucault, Michel. *The Use of Pleasure.* Trans. Robert Hurley. New York: Vintage, 1985.

Freeman, Kenneth. *Schools of Hellas.* London: MacMillan, 1922.

Fuks, Alexander. "Isokrates and the Social-Economic Situation in Greece." *Ancient Society* 3 (1972): 17–44.

Gaines, Robert. "Isokrates, EP. 6.8." *Hermes* 118 (1990): 165–70.

Garner, Richard. *Law and Society in Classical Athens.* London: Croom Helm, 1987.

Gillis, Daniel. "The Ethical Basis of Isocratean Rhetoric." *La Parola del passato* 38 (1983): 321–48.

———. "Isocrates, the *Philippos,* and the Evening of Democracy." *ATTI* 8 (1976–77): 123–33.

Giroux, Henry, et al. "The Need for Cultural Studies: Resisting Intellectuals and Oppositional Public Spheres." *Dalhousie Review* 64 (1984): 472–86.

Gronbeck, Bruce. "Gorgias on Rhetoric and Poetic: A Rehabilitation." *Southern Speech Communication Journal* 38 (1972): 27–38.

Grote, George. *A History of Greece.* London: John Murray, 1868.

Guthrie, W. K. C. *The Sophists.* Cambridge: Cambridge University Press, 1971.

Habermas, Jurgen. *Legitimation Crisis.* Trans. Thomas McCarthy. Boston: Beacon Press, 1975.

Hall, Stuart. *The Hard Road to Renewal.* London: Verso, 1988.

Halperin, David. *One Hundred Years of Homosexuality.* New York: Routledge, 1990.

Hamilton, Charles. "Greek Rhetoric and History: the Case of Isocrates." In *Arktouros: Hellenic Studies Presented to Bernard M. W. Knox,* edited by Glen W. Bowersock, Walter Burkert, and Michael C. J. Putnam, 290–98. New York: Walter de Gruyter, 1979.

Hamilton, Edith, and Huntington Cairns, eds. *The Collected Dialogues of Plato.* Princeton: Princeton University Press, 1961.

Hartog, François. *The Mirror of Herodotus: The Representation of the Other in the Writing of History.* Trans. Janet Lloyd. Berkeley: University of California Press, 1988.

Hauser, Gerard. *Introduction to Rhetorical Theory.* New York: Harper and Row, 1986.

Havelock, Eric. *The Liberal Temper in Greek Politics.* New Haven: Yale University Press, 1957.

———. *The Literate Revolution in Greece and Its Cultural Consequences.* Princeton: Princeton University Press, 1982.

Heilbrunn, Gunther. "Isocrates on Rhetoric and Power." *Hermes* 103 (1975): 154–78.

Herodotus. *Works.* Trans. A. D. Godley Harvard. London: William Heinemann, 1966.

Howland, R. L. "The Attack on Isocrates in the *Phaedrus.*" *Classical Quarterly* 31 (1937): 151–59.

Hudson-Williams, H. "Political Speeches in Athens." *Classical Quarterly* 65 (1951): 68–73.

Ijsseling, Samuel. "Isocrates and the Power of Logos." In his *Rhetoric and Philosophy in Conflict,* 18–25. The Hague: Martinus Nijhoff, 1976.

Isocrates. *Isocrates.* 3 vols. Trans. George Norlin (vols. 1–2) and LaRue Van Hook (vol. 3). London: William Heinemann, 1928, 1929, 1945.

Jaeger, Werner. *Paideia: The Ideals of Greek Culture.* 3 vols. Trans. Gilbert Highet. New York: Oxford University Press, 1971.

Jameson, Fredric. *The Political Unconscious.* Ithaca: Cornell University Press, 1981.

Jarratt, Susan. *Rereading the Sophists.* Carbondale: Southern Illinois University Press, 1991.

Jarrett, James. *The Educational Theories of the Sophists.* New York: Teachers College Press, 1969.

Jebb, R. C. *The Attic Orators from Antiphon to Isaeus.* 2nd ed. 2 vols. New York: Russell and Russell, 1962.

Johnson, R. "Isocrates' Methods of Teaching." *American Journal of Philology* 80 (1959): 25–36.

———. "A Note on the Number of Isocrates' Pupils." *American Journal of Philology* 78 (1957): 297–300.

Johnson, W. R. "Isocrates Flowering: The Rhetoric of Augustine." *Philosophy and Rhetoric* 9 (1976): 217–31.

Joint Association. *The World of Athens: An Introduction to Classical Athenian Culture.* Cambridge: Cambridge University Press, 1984.

Jones, A. H. M. *Athenian Democracy.* Baltimore: Johns Hopkins University Press, 1986.

Kennedy, George. *The Art of Persuasion in Greece.* Princeton: Princeton University Press, 1963.

———. "Isocrates' *Encomium of Helen:* A Panhellenic Document." *Transactions and Proceedings of the American Philological Association* 89 (1958): 77–83.

Kerferd, G. B. *The Sophistic Movement.* Cambridge: Cambridge University Press, 1981.

———, ed. *The Sophists and Their Legacy.* Wiesbaden: Franz Steiner, 1981.

Laclau, Ernesto, and Chantal Mouffe. *Hegemony and Socialist Strategy: Towards a Radical Democratic Politics.* New York: Verso, 1985.

Laistner, M. L. W. "The Influence of Isocrates' Political Doctrines on Some Fourth Century Men of Affairs." *Classical Weekly* 23 (March 1930): 129–31.

Leff, Michael. "In Search of Ariadne's Thread: A Review of the Research Literature on Rhetorical Theory." *Central States Speech Journal* 29 (1978): 73–91.

Lentz, Tony. *Orality and Literacy in Hellenic Greece.* Carbondale: Southern Illinois University Press, 1989.

Loraux, Nicole. *The Invention of Athens: Funeral Oration in the Classical City.* Trans. Alan Sheridan. Cambridge: Harvard University Press, 1986.

MacDowell, Douglass. *The Law in Classical Athens.* Ithaca: Cornell University Press, 1978.

Markle, Minor. "Support of Athenian Intellectuals for Philip: A Study of Isocrates' *Philippus* and Speusippus' *Letter to Philip.*" *Journal of Hellenic Studies* 96 (1976): 80–99.

Marrou, Henri. *A History of Education in Antiquity.* Trans. George Lamb. New York: Sheed and Ward, 1956.

McGee, Michael. "The Moral Problem of *Argumentum* per *Argumentum.*" In *Argument and Social Practice: Proceedings of the Fourth SCA/AFA Conference on Argumentation,* edited by Robert Cox, Malcolm Sillars, and Gregg Walker, 1–15. Annandale, Va.: SCA, 1985.

McKeon, Richard. "Uses of Rhetoric in a Technological Age: Architectonic Productive Arts." In *The Prospect of Rhetoric,* edited by Lloyd Bitzer and Edwin Black, 44–63. Englewood Cliffs, N.J.: Prentice-Hall, 1971.

McKerrow, Raymie. "Critical Rhetoric: Theory and Practice." *Communication Monographs* 56 (1989): 91–111.

Merlan, Philip. "Isocrates, Aristotle and Alexander the Great." *Historia* 3 (1954–55): 60–81.

Miller, Carolyn. "The *Polis* as Rhetorical Community." *Rhetorica* 11 (1993): 211–40.

Moss, Roger. "The Case for Sophistry." In *Rhetoric Revalued,* edited by Brian Vickers, 207–24. Binghamton, N.Y.: Center for Medieval and Early Renaissance Studies, 1982.

Moysey, Robert. "Isocrates and Chares: A Study in the Political Spectrum of Mid-Fourth Century Athens." *Ancient World* 15 (1987): 81–86.

———. "Isocrates' *On the Peace:* Rhetorical Exercise or Political Advice?" *American Journal of Ancient History* 7 (1982): 118–27.

Murphy, James. *A Synoptic History of Classical Rhetoric.* Davis, Calif.: Hermagoras Press, 1983.

Neserius, Philip. "Isocrates' Political and Social Ideas." *International Journal of Ethics* 43 (1932–33): 307–28.

North, Helen. "The Use of Poetry in the Training of the Ancient Orator." *Traditio* 8 (1952): 1–33.

Nussbaum, Martha. *Fragility of Goodness: Luck and Ethics in Greek Tragedy and Philosophy.* New York: Cambridge University Press, 1986.

Ober, Josiah. *Mass and Elite in Democratic Athens: Rhetoric, Ideology, and the Power of the People.* Princeton: Princeton University Press, 1989.

Oravec, Christine. "'Observation' in Aristotle's Theory of Epideictic." *Philosophy and Rhetoric* 9 (1976): 162–74.

Perkins, Terry. "Isocrates and Plato: Relativism vs. Idealism." *Southern Speech Communication Journal* 50 (1984): 49–66.

Perlman, S. "Isocrates' 'Philippus'—A Reinterpretation." *Historia* 6 (1957): 306–17.

———. "Panhellenism, the Polis and Imperialism." *Historia* 25 (1976): 1–30.

Plato. *Gorgias.* Trans. W. R. M. Lamb. London: William Heinemann, 1983.

———. *The Laws.* 2 vols. Trans. R. G. Bury. London: William Heinemann, 1984.

———. *Menexenus.* Trans. R. G. Bury. London: William Heinemann, 1981.

———. *Phaedrus.* Trans. Harold Fowler. London: William Heinemann, 1982.

———. *Protagoras.* Trans. W. R. M. Lamb. London: William Heinemann, 1977.

———. *Republic.* Trans. Paul Shorey. London: William Heinemann, 1982, 1987.

———. *Sophist.* Trans. Harold Fowler. London: William Heinemann, 1977.

———. *Statesman.* Trans. Harold Fowler and W. R. M. Lamb. London: William Heinemann, 1975.

Poulakos, John. "Argument, Practicality, and Eloquence in Isocrates' *Helen.*" *Rhetorica* 4 (1986): 1–19.

———. "Early Changes in Rhetorical Practice and Understanding: From the Sophists to Isocrates." *Texte* 8 (1989): 307–24.

———. "Gorgias' and Isocrates' Use of the Encomium." *Southern Speech Communication Journal* 51 (1986): 300–307.

———. "Gorgias' *Encomium to Helen* and the Defense of Rhetoric." *Rhetorica* 1 (1983): 1–19.

———. *Sophistical Rhetoric in Classical Greece.* Columbia: University of South Carolina Press, 1994.

Poulakos, Takis. "Epideictic Rhetoric as Social Hegemony: Isocrates' *Helen.*" In *Rhetoric and Ideology,* edited by Charles Kneupper, 156–66. Arlington, Texas: RSA, 1989.

―――. "Human Agency in the History of Rhetoric: Gorgias' *Encomium of Helen.*" In *Writing Histories of Rhetoric,* edited by Victor Vitanza, 59–80. Carbondale: Southern Illinois University Press, 1994.

―――. "Isocratean Rhetorical Education: A Structural Precedent for Cultural Studies." In *Rhetoric in the Vortex of Cultural Studies,* edited by Arthur Walzer, 42–50. St. Paul: RSA, 1993.

―――. "Recovering the Voices of the Text: Rhetorical Criticism as Ideological Critique." In *Argument and Critical Practices,* edited by Joseph Wenzel, 39–44. Annandale, Virginia: SCA, 1987.

―――. "Isocrates' Use of Narrative in the *Evagoras:* Epideictic Rhetoric and Moral Action." *Quarterly Journal of Speech* 73 (1987): 317–28.

―――. "Toward a Cultural Understanding of Classical Epideictic Oratory." *Pre/Text* 9 (1988): 147–66.

―――, ed. *Rethinking the History of Rhetoric: Multidisciplinary Essays on the Rhetorical Tradition.* Boulder: Westview Press, 1993.

Race, William. "Pindaric Encomium and Isokrates' *Evagoras.*" *Transactions of the American Philological Association* 117 (1987): 131–55.

Raymond, Jean-François de. "Isocrates et le langage de la culture." *Cahiers de Philosophie Ancienne* 5 (1986): 153–63.

Ricoeur, Paul. *Hermeneutics and the Human Sciences.* Edited and translated by John B. Thompson. Cambridge: Cambridge University Press, 1981.

―――. *The Rule of Metaphor.* Trans. Robert Czerny with Kathleen McLaughlin and John Costello. Toronto: University of Toronto Press, 1977.

Rosenfield, Lawrence. "The Practical Celebration of Epideictic." In *Rhetoric in Transition: Studies in the Nature and Uses of Rhetoric,* edited by Eugene White, 131–55. University Park: Pennsylvania State University Press, 1980.

Rosenmeyer, Thomas. "Gorgias, Aeschylus, and *Apate.*" *American Journal of Philology* 76 (1955): 225–60.

Rummel, Erika. "Isocrates' Ideal of Rhetoric: Criteria of Evaluation." *Classical Journal* 75 (1979): 25–35.

Schiappa, Edward. *Protagoras and Logos: A Study in Greek Philosophy and Rhetoric.* Columbia: University of South Carolina Press, 1991.

Segal, Charles. "Gorgias and the Psychology of the Logos." *Harvard Studies in Classical Philology* 66 (1962): 99–155.

Sheeks, Wayne. "Isocrates, Plato, and Xenophon against the Sophists." *The Personalist* 56 (1975): 250–59.

Sihvola, Juha. *Decay, Progress, the Good Life? Hesiod and Protagoras on the Development of Culture.* Helsinki: Finnish Society of Sciences and Letters, 1989.

Sprague, Rosamond. *The Older Sophists.* Columbia: University of South Carolina Press, 1972.

Ste Croix, G. E. M. de. *The Class Struggle in the Ancient Greek World.* Ithaca: Cornell University Press, 1981.

Stockton David. *The Classical Athenian Democracy.* Oxford: Oxford University Press, 1990.

Sutton, Jane. "Rereading Sophistical Arguments: A Political Intervention." *Argumentation* 5 (1991): 141–57.

Thompson, Wesley. "Isocrates on the Peace Treaties." *Classical Quarterly* 33 (1983): 75–80.

Thucydides. *History of the Peloponnesian War.* 4 vols. Trans. Charles Smith. London: William Heinemann, 1968.

Vatai, Frank. *Intellectuals in Politics in the Greek World.* London: Croom Helm, 1984.

Vernant, Jean-Pierre. *Myth and Thought Among the Greeks.* London: Routledge, 1983.

———. *The Origins of Greek Thought.* Ithaca: Cornell University Press, 1982.

Vickers, Brian. "Epideictic and Epic in the Renaissance." *New Literary History* 14 (1982–83): 497–537.

———. *In Defence of Rhetoric.* Oxford: Clarendon Press, 1988.

Wagner, Russell. "The Rhetorical Theory of Isocrates." *Quarterly Journal of Speech Education* 8 (1922): 323–37.

Wallace, Robert. "The Date of Isokrates' *Areopagiticus.*" *Harvard Studies in Classical Philology* 90 (1986): 77–84.

Weaver, Richard. "The *Phaedrus* and the Nature of Rhetoric." In *The Ethics of Rhetoric,* 3–26. Chicago: Henry Regnery, 1953.

Welch, Kathleen. *The Contemporary Reception of Classical Rhetoric: Appropriations of an Ancient Discourse.* Hillsdale, N.J.: Lawrence Erlbaum, 1990.

———. "Writing Instruction in Ancient Athens After 450 BC." In *A Short History of Writing Instruction,* edited by James Murphy, 1–17. Davis, Calif.: Hermagoras Press, 1990.

Welles, Bradford C. "Isocrates' View of History." In *The Classical Tradition,* edited by Luitpold Wallach, 3–25. Ithaca: Cornell University Press, 1966.

Wilcox, Stanley. "Criticisms of Isocrates and His *philosophia.*" *Transactions and Proceedings of the American Philological Association* 74 (1943): 113–33.

———. "Isocrates' Fellow-Rhetoricians." *American Journal of Philology* 66 (1945): 171–86.

———. "The Scope of Early Rhetorical Instruction." *Harvard Studies in Classical Philology* 53 (1942): 121–55.

Wood, Ellen. *Peasant-Citizen and Slave.* New York: Verso, 1988.

Index

Acropolis, 42
Aeschylus, 12–13
Against Callimachus, 19
Against the Sophists, 7, 41, 53, 75, 95–96, 99, 101
Agamemnon, 59
aido, 16–17, 22, 31
akolasia, 43
Alcibiades, 42, 44–45, 110n. 21
Alcmaeon, 100
Anderson, Perry, 110n. 1
Antidosis, 7, 31, 36–37, 39–41, 54, 56–57, 59, 60, 62, 67–71, 73, 74, 80, 86, 93–95, 97–100, 102–4, 108n. 21, 111n. 35, 112nn. 12, 14, 114n. 2
Antigone, 12
apographe, 66
archein, 41
Areopagiticus, 30, 38, 42, 44, 56, 74, 109n. 6
Aristophanes, 107n. 2, 108n. 3
Aristotle, 2, 20, 39, 64–65, 79, 114n. 11
  Art of Rhetoric, 2, 55
  Athenian Constitution, 64–65
  Politics, 39, 65
Arnheim, M. T. W., 110n. 1
Athena, 12
Athenians, 2, 5–6, 22–23, 27, 30, 33, 36, 38, 42, 46–47, 50
Athens. *See* Athenians
Attica, 59, 90
Attic orators, 1
Austin, M. M., 110n. 1

Bacchylides, 76
Barrett, Harold, 107n. 3
Baynes, Norman, 29–30, 109n. 2
Beck, Frederick, 1, 107n. 2, 109n. 4, 115n. 4
Benoit, William, 112n. 14
Bitzer, Lloyd F., 108n. 15
Blumenberg, Hans, 15, 108nn. 7, 10, 111nn. 21, 22, 113n. 20
Bonner, Robert J., 112n. 3
Burke, Kenneth, 108n. 13

Cahn, Michael, 107n. 1, 115n. 3
Callicles, 52–53, 69
Campbell, Blair, 115n. 8
Carthage, 38
Cleon, 65
Cole, Thomas, 112n. 2
Connor, W. R., 109n. 12, 110n. 1, 112n. 15
Corax, 101
Crowley, Sharon, 111n. 13
Cyprus, 27

Davidson, James, 110n. 1
Davies, John, 110n. 1
Decelea, 38
Demeter, 82
Demonicus, 41, 58
demos, 65
de Raymond, Jean-François, 112n. 14
de Romilly, Jacqueline, 111nn. 13, 19, 24, 29, 115n. 6

Derrida, Jacques, 109n. 15
De Vries, G. J., 112n. 14
Diels, Hermann, 111n. 13
dikaiosyne, 16, 28, 35–36, 41, 54
dike, 16–17, 22, 31
Dixsaut, Monique, 112n. 14
Dodds, E. R., 108n. 9
Dover, K. J., 115n. 8
doxa, 57, 80, 86–87, 97
doxastike, 96
Dubois, Page, 110n. 1
Dupreel, Eugene, 111n. 13
Durant, Will, 110n. 21

Empedocles, 100
empeiria, 95–96
Enos, Richard Leo, 112nn. 2, 11
epideixis, 77, 81, 90
epimeleia, 96
Epimetheus, 12
episteme, 86
eu legein. See *legein*
Euripides, 13
Evagoras, 41, 75–77, 111n. 37,
    113n. 24
Evagoras, 7, 41, 75–77

Farrar, Cynthia, 49, 109nn. 5, 22,
    110nn. 3, 7, 111nn. 14, 15
Farrell, Thomas, 108n. 13
Fine, John, 110nn. 11, 20
Finley, M. I., 65, 108n. 12, 110n. 1,
    112nn. 3, 12
Fisher, Walter, 108n. 13
Foucault, Michel, 58, 111n. 33
Freeman, Kenneth, 1, 107n. 2
Fuks, Alexander, 110n. 1

Gaines, Robert, 112n. 14
Garner, Richard, 112nn. 3, 8
Gillis, Daniel, 109n. 8
Giroux, Henry, 115n. 8
Gorgias, 5–6, 23, 24–25, 41, 45, 47, 50–
    52, 61, 78, 100, 102, 105, 108n. 18,
    109n. 19, 110nn. 13, 22, 23, 111n. 17,
    113n. 1

Encomium to Helen, 23, 45, 109n. 25,
    110n. 23, 114n. 12
Nonexistent, The, 24
graphe, 66
Gronbeck, Bruce, 111n. 20
Guthrie, W. K. C., 15, 108nn. 4, 17,
    109n. 24, 110nn. 6, 12, 114n. 8

Habermas, Jurgen, 108n. 13
Hall, Stuart, 107n. 12
Hauser, Gerard, 108n. 13
Havelock, Eric, 110n. 1, 113n. 2
Hegel, G. W. F., 62
Heilbrunn, Gunther, 61, 74
Helen, 59
Helen, 7, 19, 59, 60, 67, 74, 115n. 5
Hellas, 74, 83–85
Hellenes, 42–43, 75, 80, 82–84, 86, 95
Hephastus, 12
Heracles, 83
Hermes, 14
Hesiod, 76
Hippocrates, 23
Homer, 76
Hudson-Williams, H., 108n. 12
"Hymn to Logos," 5, 9–10, 11, 12–25,
    62

Ijsseling, Samuel, 107n. 6, 108n. 11
Isocrates. *See* individual works
Italy, 38

Jaeger, Werner, 1, 5, 10, 30–31, 62–63,
    107nn. 2, 10, 11, 109nn. 1, 2, 115n. 7
Jameson, Fredric, 108n. 15
Jarratt, Susan, 107n. 5
Jarrett, James, 115n. 4
Jebb, R. C., 107n. 1
Johnson, R., 109n. 3, 112n. 12
Johnson, W. R., 112n. 14
Jones, A. H. M., 108n. 12, 109n. 14,
    110n. 1, 112n. 3

kairos, 97, 115n. 3
Kennedy, George, 1, 5, 107nn. 1, 2, 10,
    109n. 3

Kerferd, G. B., 109nn. 23, 24, 110n. 6,
    111n. 13
Kleisthenes, 64
Kranz, Walter, 111n. 13
kyrios, 109n. 16

Lacedaemonians, 38, 42, 44, 81, 83–84
Laclau, Ernesto, 107n. 12
Laistner, M. L. W., 110n. 1
Leff, Michael, 108n. 13
legein, 64–65, 66, 68–71, 72, 74, 79,
    80
Lentz, Tony, 113nn. 16, 19
Lysias, 109n. 18

MacDowell, Douglas, 112nn. 3, 9,
    10
Marathon, 83
Marrou, Henri, 1, 107nn. 2, 10,
    109nn. 3, 4
McGee, Michael, 2, 107n. 7, 111n. 30
McKeon, Richard, 108n. 13
McKerrow, Rymie, 108n. 13
Melissus, 100
Moss, Roger, 107n. 5
Mouffe, Chantal, 107n. 12
Moysey, Robert, 110n. 1, 114n. 7
Murphy, James, 108n. 13
Mytilinean(s), 72

Nesarius, Philip, 109n. 9
Nicocles, 26, 27–29, 31–32, 34, 35, 39,
    41, 60, 75–77, 93
Nicocles, 6, 9, 11, 19–20, 26–27, 29–31,
    34, 71
Norlin, George, 79, 111n. 27, 113n. 1
Nussbaum, Martha, 109n. 18, 111nn.
    23, 25, 32, 114nn. 4, 11

Ober, Josiah, 109nn. 10, 11, 17, 110n. 2,
    112nn. 2, 7
oikein, 17
oikos, 17
Olympia, 78
On the Peace, 19, 30, 36–37, 39–45, 57,
    58, 60, 74

paideia, 62
paideusis, 87, 95
Panathenaicus, 19, 38, 39, 42, 45, 60,
    69, 74, 80, 98, 99, 101, 103,
    113n. 2
Panegyricus, 7, 13, 19, 59–60, 62, 70,
    72, 74, 77–81, 83–84, 86, 88–90,
    108n. 13, 111n. 26, 113n. 1, 114n. 7,
    115n. 7
Panhellenic, 19–20, 78, 86, 88,
    113n. 1
paraphronein, 44
paraphronon, 43
Parmenides, 100
patris (patrida), 84
Peace. See On the Peace
peitho, 56
Peloponnesian War(s), 38, 64
Peloponnesus, 43
Pericles, 33, 53, 64–65
Perkins, Terry, 112n. 15
Perlman, S., 110n. 1, 114nn. 6, 7, 10
Persians, 88–89, 92
Persian Wars, 82
phasis, 66
Philip of Macedonia, 29–30, 34, 42, 44,
    59–60, 114n. 7
Philip, 42, 44, 59, 60
phronein, 44, 68–74, 79, 80, 89–90
phronesin, 86
phronesis, 79–80, 89
physis, 87, 95
Pindar, 76
Plato, 1–2, 4–5, 14–16, 18, 23–24, 36,
    37, 40, 48, 52–53, 56, 63, 66–67, 69,
    108nn. 14, 19, 111nn. 16, 25, 28,
    112n. 15
    Gorgias, 10, 41, 45, 52, 109nn. 13, 19,
        111n. 16
    Phaedrus, 23, 56, 108n. 14, 109n. 18,
        111nn. 25, 32
    Protagoras, 12, 14, 23, 31–32, 35, 48,
        110n. 10
    Theaetetus, 15
Poulakos, John, 2, 108nn. 11, 19,
    110n. 9, 111n. 17, 112n. 14

Poulakos, Takis, 2–5, 7, 22, 30, 49, 56, 62, 84, 104, 107nn. 8, 9, 111n. 26, 113nn. 18, 24, 114n. 1
Prometheus, 11–12, 15–16
Protagoras, 5–6, 12, 14–18, 22–25, 32, 35, 47–50, 53, 61, 105, 108n. 20, 109nn. 5, 22, 110nn. 4, 8, 10
psyche, 96

Ricoeur, Paul, 108n. 13
Rummel, Erika, 112n. 14

Schiappa, Edward, 109n. 5, 110nn. 4, 5
Segal, Charles, 108n. 18, 109n. 25, 110n. 22, 111n. 18
Sheeks, Wayne, 112n. 15
Sicily, 38
Sihvola, Juha, 108nn. 5, 9, 20
Socrates, 14–15, 35, 48–49, 52, 109n. 18
Sophists, The, 1–2, 15, 23, 27, 32, 63, 88, 108n. 19, 111n. 13
Sophocles, 12–13
sophron, 43
sophrosyne, 16, 28, 35–36, 41–43, 54, 57
Sparta, 42, 83–85
Sprague, Rosamond, 108n. 17, 110n. 13
Stockton, David, 110n. 1, 112nn. 3, 4, 5
Suppliants, 108n. 8
Sutton, Jane, 111n. 13
sycophants, 66

tarache, 42–45, 56, 110n. 22
Thebes, 83
Theognis, 76

Thermopylae, 83
Theseus, 59
Thompson, Wesley, 110n. 1
Thrasymachus, 23, 108n. 17
    Constitution, The, 23
Thucydides, 72, 78, 107n. 2
Timotheus, 93, 102–3, 111n. 35
Tisias, 101
To Demonicus, 69
To Nicocles, 26–27, 37, 41, 72–74, 76, 94
To Philip, 29
To Timotheus, 37
Trapeziticus, 19
Trojans, 59, 91
Trojan War, 82
Troy. *See* Trojans
tyche, 80, 114n. 11
tyrannein, 41

Van Hook, LaRue, 79
Vatai, Frank, 110n. 1, 114n. 7
Vernant, Jean-Pierre, 65, 108n. 16, 112nn. 3, 6
Vickers, Brian, 107n. 3, 108n. 13
Vidal-Naquet, P., 110n. 1

Wagner, Russel, 112n. 14
Weaver, Richard, 111n. 31
Welch, Katleen, 107nn. 6, 10
Wilcox, Stanley, 108n. 12, 112n. 12, 113n. 15

Zeus, 14–15, 17, 59